THE
MARRIAGE COUNSELING
WORKBOOK

THE MARRIAGE COUNSELING WORKBOOK

8 STEPS TO A STRONG AND LASTING RELATIONSHIP

EMILY COOK, PHD, LCMFT

ALTHEA PRESS

To my clients
past, present, and future

CONTENTS

INTRODUCTION

MARRIAGE COUNSELING IS BOTH A SCIENCE AND AN ART. It is most effective when both partners are committed to each other, willing to make an all-out effort to improve their relationship through therapy, and are working with a competent and experienced marriage-counseling specialist. This workbook offers a peek into what good, effective marriage counseling is like. I've combined my specific clinical training as a licensed marriage and family therapist with my years of private practice experience counseling couples to provide you with practical wisdom and in-depth exercises that will help you repair and enrich your relationship.

My guess is that things are pretty hard right now. Maybe you're a newlywed who is tasting the bitter flavor of hurtful conflict or emotional hardship for the first time. Maybe you've been married for a few years and are struggling with difficult circumstances, like meddling in-laws or betrayal. Or maybe you woke up one day to find that the person you've been married to for the better part of your life is somewhat of a stranger. What has happened in your marriage and how you feel about your partner and what you want for your married future are details only you know. Your story is unique. But whether you're despairing about your marriage and desperate for change, or only *just* uncomfortable enough to seek self-help support, this workbook is designed for *you*.

This workbook is purposefully focused on the classic, fundamental problems that troubled marriages face. It shows you the way forward to reconnecting with your partner in sequential steps you can complete at your own pace. Although it's best that both partners work together, you can use this workbook without your partner's participation—one is better than neither trying to strengthen a marriage.

Like a stone thrown into a pond, the changes you make will ripple through the marriage.

The couples who have come into my office have benefited from the practical help you'll find in this workbook. In this step-by-step program, you'll identify what is causing you pain in your marriage, learn how to alleviate it, and confidently prevent it in the future. The content of each chapter is similar to what you'd encounter in a course of marriage counseling with me, so you're about to embark on a self-directed marriage-counseling journey. Go at the pace that feels right to you and your partner, but keep momentum going and stick with it.

The book is divided into two parts. The two chapters in the first part explore the conflicts you're facing now and the factors that have shaped your marriage. In chapter 1, you'll learn about the common problems married couples face and assess your own relationship. In chapter 2, you'll discover the ways your past influences your present by exploring your family of origin, your previous romantic relationships, and your early marriage history.

The second part of the book presents an eight-step program for reconnecting with your partner. Each step builds on the one before it, so even if certain steps resonate more than others, it's important to work through the entire program. The steps that may already be an area of relationship strength will give you positive momentum in the steps that are more challenging. And each step provides you with a new tool to heal and strengthen your marriage, along with many interactive opportunities to practice the skills and make positive changes.

Step 1 is "Communicate Effectively." Communication is the foundation of all relationships. In this step, you'll improve your ability to communicate with love and respect. Financial issues often top the list of reasons couples fight, so in step 2, "Face Finances," you'll learn what these fights actually mean and how to resolve them. And those new communication skills will be especially important for the discussions and exercises in step 3, "Explore Intimacy." Step 4 is when you'll "Reunite as *We*," reestablishing your relationship to the highest level of priority without sacrificing your individuality.

In step 5, "Build Trust," you'll explore the big and small ways partners undermine trust in one another and learn how to repair the damage. Step 6, "Revisit Family," helps you identify and relieve the parenting and family stressors that

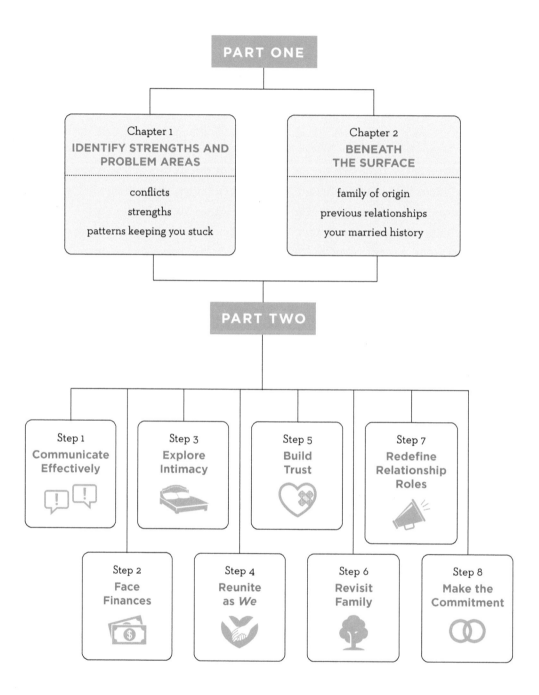

PART ONE

Chapter 1
IDENTIFY STRENGTHS AND PROBLEM AREAS

conflicts

strengths

patterns keeping you stuck

Chapter 2
BENEATH THE SURFACE

family of origin

previous relationships

your married history

PART TWO

Step 1
Communicate Effectively

Step 2
Face Finances

Step 3
Explore Intimacy

Step 4
Reunite as *We*

Step 5
Build Trust

Step 6
Revisit Family

Step 7
Redefine Relationship Roles

Step 8
Make the Commitment

strain your marriage. An imbalance in household equality often causes resentment and conflict, so in step 7, "Redefine Relationship Roles," you'll learn how to improve your teamwork. And finally, step 8 is where you'll "Make the Commitment" to a long-lasting married future that is healthy and strong.

As you get to know your own marriage, you'll also get to know the marriages of four couples who, by example, will show you how to apply what you're learning: Josh and Heather, Carlos and Janelle, Beth and Mei-Lin, and Tim and Linda. These couples are composites of real men and women I've counseled in my practice, merged together both to protect their identities and to provide rich illustrations of the common experiences of marital conflict.

Here's what I expect from you, the partner and the couple:

- An open mind and creative approach to new ideas and relationship skills
- A willingness to be honest about your feelings, opinions, desires, and concerns
- A readiness to hear what your partner has to share about their experiences
- Motivation to bring your authentic self to this work
- Dedication to complete the entire program without giving up on the workbook or your marriage

And here's what you can expect from me, your marriage counselor:

- Reassurance that you are not alone in your pain
- A sincere belief in your ability to overcome problems through effort and good humor
- Guidance toward a deeper understanding of your relationship patterns and how your past influences your present
- Practical strategies to help you reconnect with your partner and initiate a positive married future
- Encouragement to stick with the program, even when it's difficult

No matter how you're feeling right now—hopeful, anxious, hurt, frustrated, tired, ready for change—I'll be with you every step of the way. My deepest hope for you is that this workbook helps you restore your marriage to a place of health and connection, and encourages you to interact with your partner with a renewed sense of emotional safety and playful fun.

HOW TO USE THIS WORKBOOK

Chapters include exercises, many of which are writing prompts. Freewrite your answers without judging or editing your responses. When completing exercises with your partner, one of you can respond directly in the workbook and the other may use a journal. If the partner using the workbook needs more space to answer the questions, they can continue in a separate journal. Keep these journals together with the workbook so you can refer back to them.

When responding to a quiz, keep track of your individual responses by circling your answers in different colors. Do the same with activities that you both complete together. But remember which color belongs to whom!

After any exercise is complete, discuss your answers and feelings with each other to explore your perspectives on the topic. It may be helpful to take conversation notes, either in the workbook or in one of the journals. These conversations will help deepen understanding and bridge your separate experiences with the workbook and its material.

PART 1

BEGIN AT THE BEGINNING

Effective marriage counseling is a delicate balancing act—first and foremost, your therapist must help two distinct individuals with unique experiences feel heard while also offering support in service of the marriage. Chapter 1 helps you and your partner assess your relationship's problem areas and strengths, and your individual styles of solving conflict. Then, it guides you through sharing your perspectives to find common ground and set shared goals for your married future.

Effective marriage counseling must also balance the past, present, and future—always helping the couple make links between where they've come from and where they want to go to improve their experience of the now. This is the focus of chapter 2. We'll look backward at the relationships that shaped your families growing up and the relationships that shaped your dating histories. We'll also pay attention to the circumstances and relationship patterns that shaped the beginning of your marriage. Then you'll learn what these factors mean, and you'll come to understand the historical forces currently influencing your marriage.

With a deeper understanding of your past, and by applying what you learn to the present problems in your marriage, you will be able to make more informed choices about the strategies I offer in part 2. To help you along the way, I've woven in the stories of four couples throughout this workbook. Here is a brief introduction to each couple:

JOSH AND HEATHER

Married for 8 years, together for 12 years. College sweethearts, got married in their early twenties after graduation. They have a four-year-old son, Mason, and a one-year-old daughter, Lucy. They live in the suburbs. Josh works in finance, travels frequently for work, and often works late hours. Heather worked as a human resources manager at a large company until Lucy was born, and she is having difficulty adjusting to life as a stay-at-home mom.

CARLOS AND JANELLE

Married for 2 years, together for 4 years. Met through a dating app, both in their early thirties. Carlos is a high school world studies teacher. Janelle is a policy analyst for a think tank. Carlos comes from a modest family background and is a middle child of three; Janelle comes from a wealthy family and is an only child. They live in a city loft that Janelle's parents helped them buy, in the same city where her parents live. Carlos's family is an airplane flight away. They want kids, but Janelle may have fertility issues.

BETH AND MEI-LIN

Unmarried, together for 10 years. Met at an art museum where they both still work. They had a private commitment ceremony at year five and are ready to get legally married now. Beth is outgoing and wants a big celebration, while Mei-Lin is more reserved and wants an intimate ceremony. Mei-Lin has mild depression and anxiety but takes medication and sees a counselor. Beth is a heavy social drinker and likes to party. They live in a city town house they renovated together, and they have two cats. They met while Beth was in a relationship with Clara. Beth cheated on Clara with Mei-Lin, which ended her relationship with Clara.

TIM AND LINDA

Married for 30 years. Met in graduate school where Linda majored in mathematics and Tim in construction management. They just celebrated their anniversary with an intimate party of family and friends. Linda has been a stay-at-home mom the whole marriage, and now that their kids are launching, she wants to work part-time teaching at a community college. Tim owns a construction company with his brother. He is ready to pass business operations to his brother and wants to travel and play golf. They have two sons, Anthony and Michael, and an adopted daughter, Sabrina. Sabrina recently transitioned from community college and living at home to a four-year college in another state. Anthony lives in the same city as his parents and recently got engaged. Michael is serving in the Peace Corps in South America.

CHAPTER 1

IDENTIFY YOUR STRENGTHS AND PROBLEM AREAS

Good news: you're not alone! All couples have problems. That couple holding hands on the subway train? They fight about money! That couple laughing at the bar? They fight about who does more chores around the house! That couple sitting on the bleachers watching their child play soccer? They fight about not having enough sex! So before you dive in to this chapter's assessment of your marriage's strengths and problem areas, I want you to know that you are not alone in your experience of relationship conflict.

Relationship conflict stems from many factors. Two people navigating their own lives and a shared life together are bound to disagree sometimes. Two people who grew up in different types of families are bound to make different assumptions about what marriage and family should feel like. And two people who are committed to each other in Western culture are bound to be influenced by the fairy tale of happily ever after and disappointed when marriage turns out to be harder than they anticipated.

With some effort, most marital problems are solvable. But before we get to the work of restoring your marriage and reconnecting with your partner, you need to become familiar with the common problem areas of marriage so you can focus on the issues that affect you the most.

In this chapter, you and your partner will develop a deeper understanding of the problems you're facing by learning about your areas of conflict, areas of strength, and patterns of interacting with each other. This assessment will help you come to a common understanding of your struggles, and the information will, in later chapters, inform a vision statement for your future.

This workbook is not intended for marriages that are abusive in any way. In fact, putting yourself in the vulnerable position of working on your relationship could expose you to further harm. Abuse in marriage can come in many forms: emotional, psychological, physical, sexual, or possessive. It can be pervasive or happen one time. It can seem mild enough to tolerate (False! No amount of relationship violence is acceptable!) or severe enough to necessitate ending the relationship (True! You deserve to be safe in all ways!). Turn to appendix B on page 248 to assess your marriage for abuse.

Three Common Myths about Marriage

Most couples start out with high expectations for a strong, happy, and healthy marriage. And then life gets going, and day-to-day realities or difficult circumstances begin to deflate—or even burst—that bubble. In the following exercises, challenge your belief in three common marriage myths. Then, take action in your marriage to demonstrate the power of myth busting.

MYTH #1: I ALREADY KNOW EVERYTHING ABOUT MY PARTNER AND MYSELF.

Beth is tempted to believe this myth, but Mei-Lin isn't so sure. Beth says, "I'm pretty sure I know Mei-Lin the best of anyone—sometimes better than she knows herself." Mei-Lin says, "But sometimes that means you assume I need one thing, when I'd prefer another. Like when you don't invite me out to drinks after work because you think I'd rather just go home. Sometimes, I do want to go."

Are you tempted to believe Myth #1? Why or why not?

_____

_____

_____

_____

BUST THIS MYTH

Myth #1 is an example of rigid thinking, which prevents openness to growth and stifles your ability to think creatively about solving disagreements. Sure, you know your partner really well, and this is a good thing! Knowing about your partner means your relationship is built on friendship, intimacy, and familiarity. But a healthy marriage also requires flexibility in your thinking, willingness to learn new things as each of you grows and changes, and paying attention to each other. So the same thing goes for learning about yourself! It's important not to let old assumptions get in the way of curiosity.

Take turns asking each other these questions, and then discuss your answers using the prompts below.

1 What do you consider your dream job?
2 What was the best thing that happened to you in the last year?
3 If you could travel anywhere in the world for five weeks, where would you go?
4 What are your most and least favorite foods?
5 How do you feel about current world events?

Did you learn anything new about your partner? Did your partner learn anything new about you? Did each of you discover something new about yourselves?

_____

_____

_____

_____

MYTH #2: LOVE IS ALL WE NEED.

Tim and Linda both recognize the trap of this myth. Linda asks, "Do you think we got lazy about actively showing love? I do, especially when I think about the years the kids were younger." Tim replies, "I think so. Sometimes when I would have the idea to do something extra nice, like buy you flowers, I'd end up just driving right past the shop. I'd tell myself, 'She already knows I love her.'" Linda replies, "I would have appreciated flowers." And Tim says, "I would have appreciated sex!"

EXPLORE THIS MYTH

Are you tempted to believe Myth #2? Why or why not?

_____

_____

_____

_____

BUST THIS MYTH

If you're tempted to believe Myth #2, you're probably feeling disappointed. When love is all you need and you already love each other, you're likely to put your relationship on autopilot. Instead, a healthy marriage requires you to intentionally cultivate active love—that is, do loving acts. And anyway, your love for each other isn't likely the problem; it's how you treat each other, how you get along, how you function as a team, and how you plan for the future. Be careful—believing in this myth may make you vulnerable to living with bad behavior. Love is not a reason to tolerate disrespect.

Do you rely on love alone to get your marriage through tough times? What are the qualities besides love that are important in your marriage? Rank the following 10 marriage values in order of priority to you. You can also add a few of your own. Then, compare your lists with your partner.

_____ Commitment   _____ Playfulness

_____ Forgiveness   _____ Respect

_____ Friendship   _____ Shared vision of the future

_____ Kindness   _____ Skills for managing conflict

_____ Passion   _____ Teamwork

_____

_____

_____

_____

MYTH #3: IF I HAVE TO ASK, IT'S MEANINGLESS.

"I definitely catch myself believing this one," says Heather. "Because Josh works out of the house, his schedule allows for alone time that he can use for going to the gym or meeting friends for drinks. I desperately want him to offer to help me do those things too, but I don't ask. I want him to offer." "Just tell me when you need me to be home so you can go out with your friends, and I'll figure it out," says Josh. "Never mind," replies Heather.

Are you tempted to believe Myth #3? Why or why not?

_____

_____

_____

_____

BUST THIS MYTH

This myth is a root of the most common communication problems and conflict-resolution impasses couples face. That's because it's linked to several other related myths, like "My partner can read my mind and know what I need without me asking." This is false! Your partner may be an amazing person, but that doesn't give them the superpower of mind reading. Another related myth is "Spontaneous acts of kindness are more valuable than fulfilled requests." This is also false! Both types of kindness are important in a marriage; neither is more valuable than the other. The ability to ask for what you need in your relationship is assertiveness, a quality that comes from self-confidence and self-worth.

Are you having trouble asking for what you want from your partner? Take turns using the following prompts to ask your partner for something you'd like more or less of in your marriage:

I'd like to ask for more/less _____.

It's meaningful to me because _____.

When this happens, I'll feel _____.

I'll show you that I'm grateful by _____.

Everyday Issues

Most couples argue about similar types of issues. The content of marital conflict can range from the mundane, like divvying up household chores, to the significant, like how to discipline children. It's also helpful to think about conflict in terms of relationship *pain*, such as whether it is mild or severe, acute or chronic.

A mild conflict might mean you argue for a few minutes and then come to a resolution or understanding quickly, whereas a more severe conflict might end with someone sleeping on the couch. Acute relationship conflict begins suddenly, feels sharp and stinging, and yet disappears when the underlying cause has been resolved. Chronic relationship conflict persists, despite the fact that the original injury may have healed.

Assessing your relationship for areas of conflict and areas of strength helps you and your partner grasp the full picture of what you're facing in your marriage. Review the following list of 40 of the most common everyday issues married couples face, and mark whether each is an area of conflict or strength in your relationship. Some of them are skills and some of them are topic areas. For those areas that cause conflict for you, think about whether it's mild or severe, or an acute or chronic problem.

Each issue is grouped into one of the Eight Steps so you can identify which step needs particular attention later in the workbook. Complete this exercise without showing each other your answers until prompted. Feel free to copy the table below for your partner.

Here's an example to help you get started:

Issue: Spending Habits

- "We're usually on the same page when it comes to spending." = Strength
- "One of us is more of a spender than the other, and it causes problems for us." = Conflict
- "We have some disagreements about spending, but we usually problem solve quickly." = Mild

- "When we fight about spending, it goes downhill fast and takes us days to recover." = Severe
- "We had a blowup about it once, but figured out a budget we more or less stick to." = Acute
- "Spending habits are an ongoing point of contention; even when we aren't fighting about it, it's there." = Chronic

IDENTIFY YOUR EVERYDAY ISSUES

Using check marks, indicate whether each issue is a strength or conflict area. For each conflict area, indicate whether it is mild or severe, acute or chronic.

	Strength Area	Conflict Area	Mild or Severe?	Acute or Chronic?
STEP 1: COMMUNICATION				
Expressing empathy				
Feeling heard and understood				
Compromise				
Fighting fair				
Avoiding conflict				
STEP 2: FINANCES				
Spending habits				
Saving habits				
Budget priorities				
Merging money/joint accounts				
Debt				

continued

	Strength Area	Conflict Area	Mild or Severe?	Acute or Chronic?
STEP 3: INTIMACY				
Satisfaction				
Frequency				
Desire				
Affection				
Emotional intimacy				
STEP 4: PARTNERSHIP				
Social styles				
Friends' opinions/influence				
Balancing time together and apart				
Having fun together				
Role of technology				
STEP 5: TRUST				
Repairing connection after a fight				
Forgiveness				
Betrayals				
Health and wellness habits (food, exercise, self-care)				
Addiction or destructive habits				

	Strength Area	Conflict Area	Mild or Severe?	Acute or Chronic?
STEP 6: FAMILY				
Your parents' opinions/influence				
Your in-laws' opinions/influences				
Parenting styles				
Reactivity				
Attachment styles				
STEP 7: RELATIONSHIP ROLES				
Household chores				
Childcare				
Work/life balance				
Coping with stress				
Teamwork				
STEP 8: COMMITMENT				
Personality differences				
Mental health issues				
Shared vision of the future				
Making decisions				
Rituals of connection				

Rank the five relationship strength areas you are most proud of, and note which of the Eight Steps will help you solidify and build on these skills. Then, rank the five areas of relationship conflict that are most distressing to you, and note which of the Eight Steps will provide focused help.

Top 5 Strengths

1 _____ Focus on step _____
2 _____ Focus on step _____
3 _____ Focus on step _____
4 _____ Focus on step _____
5 _____ Focus on step _____

Top 5 Conflicts

1 _____ Focus on step _____
2 _____ Focus on step _____
3 _____ Focus on step _____
4 _____ Focus on step _____
5 _____ Focus on step _____

MAP YOUR ISSUES

It's important to pay attention to the issues that are important to your partner, even if you don't see them as problems. Valuing your partner's perspective fosters trust, respect, and teamwork, a sense of "We're in this marriage together."

In this exercise, you and your partner will first share your top five strengths and conflict areas with each other and then map them into the Venn diagram on the next page. Use four colors to differentiate between your answers, either strength or conflict area, and your partner's answers. You'll be able to clearly see where your experiences of your marriage are unique and where they overlap.

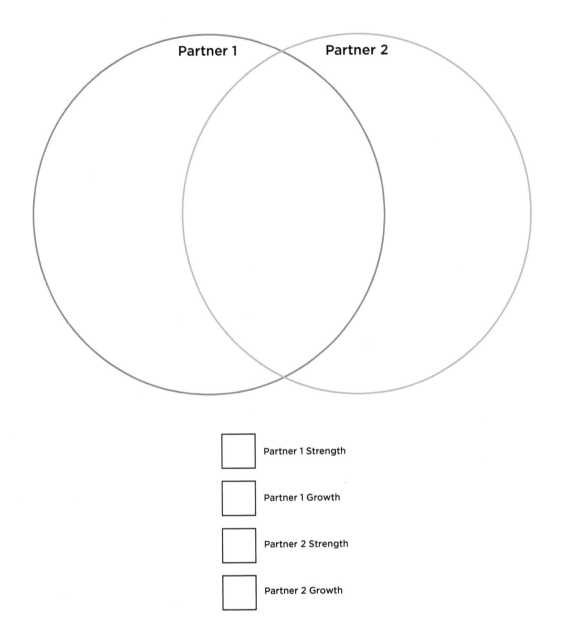

Partner 1   Partner 2

☐ Partner 1 Strength

☐ Partner 1 Growth

☐ Partner 2 Strength

☐ Partner 2 Growth

In your Venn diagram, what proportion of your answers are the same, and what proportion are different?

_____

_____

_____

_____

Does your partner's perspective on marital strengths and conflict areas surprise you?

_____

_____

_____

_____

How did each of you *feel* while filling out the diagram? (For help with identifying your feelings, see appendix A.)

_____

_____

_____

_____

How well did you communicate through this exercise?

_____

_____

_____

_____

Assessing for Sabotage

In my work with couples, I always assess for ways that partners sabotage even the best efforts to reconnect with each other. Certain types of feelings or behaviors can be poisonous to your marriage. The good news is that there are healing cures that will counteract the damage done by the poison and help restore health to your marriage.

CHECKLIST OF POISONS AND CURES

Assess your relationship for the 10 most common forms of poison and the 10 most powerful cures. Place a check mark beside any of the poisons you think might be sabotaging your marriage. Do the same for the list of cures you think might be helping your marriage.

Poisons

- ☐ Contempt
- ☐ Criticism
- ☐ Defensiveness
- ☐ Discrediting thoughts or feelings
- ☐ Holding a grudge

- ☐ Impatience
- ☐ Lack of empathy
- ☐ Rage
- ☐ Resentment
- ☐ Stonewalling

Cures

- ☐ Benefit of the doubt
- ☐ Empathy
- ☐ Forgiveness
- ☐ Kindness
- ☐ Patience

- ☐ Perspective taking
- ☐ Playfulness
- ☐ Positive regard
- ☐ Sensitivity
- ☐ Validation

NOTICE POISONS AND USE CURES

Over the next two days, commit yourself to paying attention to when you might be tempted to pour one of these poisons into your marriage. Instead, choose one of the cures to apply. Then check in with yourself:

In which situations were you tempted to use a relationship poison?

_____

_____

_____

_____

In those moments, what do you imagine your partner was feeling?

_____

_____

_____

_____

When you used a relationship cure instead, did you notice any changes in your feelings or thoughts?

_____

_____

_____

_____

How did your partner respond to the cure you used?

_____

_____

_____

_____

The Bigger Picture

In the following sections, you'll read about four common ways couples describe the bigger picture of their conflicts, illustrated by each of our four example couples. Each statement is accompanied by an exercise to write about what resonates with you and to think of examples from your own marriage. At the end, you'll have the chance to sum up the problems facing your marriage in your own words.

"WE DON'T UNDERSTAND EACH OTHER."

Overhearing Carlos and Janelle having an argument is like listening to a train go off the rails: Their communication is clearly broken. They constantly interrupt each other, and instead of listening, each is already preparing their retort. Conversations never go anywhere, because either the original issue gets lost amid complaints about how they're talking to each other or the original issue blows up into all the issues at once. They also don't have reliable or effective ways to repair after a fight or misunderstanding. Rarely does either feel heard or understood.

EXPLORE THIS CONFLICT

Do you and/or your partner feel misunderstood by the other? If so, in what types of situations does this usually occur?

_____

_____

_____

_____

"WE DON'T HAVE ANY FUN ANYMORE."

Tim and Linda are in a rut. After years of not making date night or no-kids time a priority, they've settled into routines and schedules that don't stimulate connection or sex. When they do go out together, they choose the same old restaurants or outings without a sense of newness or adventure. Although they may not admit it, sometimes they avoid spending time together because they're not sure what to talk about. They're simultaneously busy and bored.

Do you and your partner still have fun, or is it missing from your time together?

_____

_____

_____

_____

"WE'RE NOT TREATING EACH OTHER WELL."

For Josh and Heather, painful feelings of loneliness and hurt often get expressed as anger and resentment. Sometimes it's subtle, like when Josh stays late at work even though he knows Heather needs his help with the kids' bedtime . . . and even though he doesn't really need to work late that night. And sometimes it's explicit, like when Heather complains about Josh to her mom over the phone even though he can hear her from the next room. Both acknowledge that being passive-aggressive, criticizing or undermining each other, and holding on to anger by refusing to forgive are doing damage to their marriage. But both are feeling hopeless about how to change things, and the pervasive sense of negativity feels global.

EXPLORE THIS CONFLICT

Do you and/or your partner treat each other poorly? What efforts do you make to treat each other with kindness?

_____

_____

_____

_____

"WE FIGHT ABOUT EVERYTHING."

Although the content of Beth and Mei-Lin's fights may change—what to watch on TV, whose turn it is to change the litter box, whether to go out for dinner or stay in, where to go on vacation next summer—the fighting itself seems to never stop. They're stuck in a cycle of power struggles, keeping score, and bickering that is unpleasant for everyone. Their friends jokingly call them the "old married couple," but the image isn't a happy one. Mei-Lin wonders if Beth disagrees with her sometimes just for the fun of it, especially if she's been drinking. Beth wonders if Mei-Lin is too sensitive and too different from the debate-loving family she grew up in.

EXPLORE THIS CONFLICT

Do you and your partner tend to fight about everything? Are there issues that don't cause problems?

_____

_____

_____

_____

SUM UP YOUR MARRIAGE PROBLEMS

In your own words, how would you sum up your marriage problems?

_____

_____

_____

_____

Similar to the couples' examples given, how would you tell the story about those problems in your marriage?

_____

_____

_____

_____

Share your "sum up" statement and "story" with your partner. What are the differences and similarities between your and your partner's responses?

_____

_____

_____

_____

Recurring Arguments

If your marriage is like most, you probably find yourselves fighting about the same issues. Sometimes, recurring arguments happen because the first attempts at a resolution miss the mark. Once a sustainable solution is found, even if it takes some trial and error, the arguments stop. But other times, recurring arguments happen because you're trying to solve a problem that is basically unsolvable. There's no need to get discouraged here—just because a problem is unsolvable doesn't mean you have to argue about it forever!

Most problems couples face can be separated into two parts: the solvable and the unsolvable. Solvable parts of problems are the pieces you can control; they're the situational details that can be changed. Unsolvable parts of problems are the factors you can't change, like personality traits or lifestyle differences. And often when you do attempt to "solve" those fundamental parts of each other, the qualities that make you unique individuals, you feel like you're spinning your wheels. As partners we yearn for acceptance, and when we feel like our partner is trying to change who we are, we usually get defensive and perhaps even more entrenched.

So the strategy is to separate out the pieces: Problem solve together the parts you can control (Beth and Mei-Lin agree to take turns emptying the recycle bin), accept and let go of the parts you can't change (when Beth's forgetfulness gets the better of her, Mei-Lin can choose a gentle reminder rather than a sharp reprimand).

The skills needed for the solvable parts are compromise, brainstorming, and setting common goals. The skills needed for the unsolvable parts are acceptance, empathy, and perspective taking.

Here are two more examples from our couples:

Before having kids, Josh and Heather loved their lazy Saturday mornings. Josh would make coffee, Heather would fix breakfast, and they'd lounge around reading the newspaper. But now, without fail, Saturday mornings are hectic and feature the same fight over leaving on time for Mason's soccer practice at the local park.

Solvable parts: who sets the cleats and shin guards by the door, what time to start getting dressed, whether to walk to the park or drive, and so on.

Unsolvable parts: Heather is punctual and prefers to arrive at places early, but Josh doesn't mind arriving a few minutes late. Mason is easily distracted while getting ready.

When Carlos and Janelle were dating and each lived in their own apartment, neither had major complaints about the tidiness of the other person's place. But now that they live together, they fight almost every week when it's time to clean their condo.

Solvable parts: who scrubs the shower and who vacuums the rugs, which product to use on the countertops, whether to clean a little bit every day or do a marathon clean on Sunday mornings, and so forth.

Unsolvable parts: Janelle is detail oriented and feels stressed when her living space is messy. Carlos follows directions well but isn't a self-starter.

DIAGNOSE YOUR RECURRING ARGUMENTS

Use this worksheet to separate your recurring arguments into solvable and unsolvable parts:

Describe a recurring argument.	What are the solvable parts? The parts you can change?	What are the unsolvable parts? The parts you need to accept?
1 _____	1 _____	1 _____
_____	_____	_____
_____	_____	_____
_____	_____	_____
_____	_____	_____
_____	_____	_____
_____	_____	_____
2 _____	2 _____	2 _____
_____	_____	_____
_____	_____	_____
_____	_____	_____
_____	_____	_____
3 _____	3 _____	3 _____
_____	_____	_____
_____	_____	_____
_____	_____	_____
_____	_____	_____

HOW TO FIGHT FAIR

Fights can be healthy in a relationship, as long as they're fought fairly. Here are the top five rules:

1. **Give the conversation your full attention.** Put down your phone, stop doing the dishes, and turn off the TV. Face each other so you can make eye contact and touch each other by holding hands or intertwining your feet. It's much more difficult to say hurtful things when you're touching!

2. **Lead with the positive.** Expressing gratitude and acknowledging the good qualities helps disarm defensiveness. Your partner will feel appreciated, and they will see that the good things they're doing don't go unnoticed.

3. **Use active listening.** *Active listening* is a specific communication skill that slows the conversation. Because you take turns speaking and validating, your discussion is less likely to devolve into a fight. (You'll learn much more about active listening in step 1.)

4. **Take time-outs.** When conflicts escalate, you're likely to say or do something hurtful that you'll regret. Instead, as soon as one of you notices things getting heated, ask for a break. Use the time apart to self-soothe and recover from the emotional intensity. Then return to the conversation when you're both ready to try again, calmly and more productively. (You'll learn more about time-outs in step 5.)

5. **Speak with love.** Remember—you love this person! Don't assassinate your partner's character or discredit your partner's position. Treat each other with dignity and pay attention to your tone of voice. Talk to each other like you love each other, especially when you disagree.

REVIEW AND DISCUSS FIGHTING FAIR

Review the top five rules for fighting fair with your partner and have a discussion about them.

Which of these do you already do well?

_____

_____

_____

_____

Which of these does your partner do well?

_____

_____

_____

_____

Which ones do each of you need to pay more attention to?

_____

_____

_____

_____

Putting It Together

Have you ever scooped up a handful of sand at the beach? The key to keeping the sand intact in your hand is to balance a tight grasp with a loose hold, to cup your hand just enough that the sand is protected but not hard enough that it escapes.

This is what we must do with our partners. We must find the way to hold them close enough that they feel a sense of belonging, but not so close that they feel stifled. We must find the way to give them enough space that they feel free to explore the world, but not so distant that they feel unwanted.

Take a few minutes to flip back to the beginning of the chapter and review the material. Read over your answers to each exercise and refresh your memory about your discussions. No matter how things went for you, here's what I want you to know:

If you're thinking, *We're not doing as bad as I thought,* you're probably feeling pretty good. Remember to be prepared for the possibility of uncovering other areas of disconnection as you proceed through the workbook with your partner. But for now, keep up the positive momentum!

If you're thinking, *Hmm . . . we definitely have work to do, but I guess I already knew that,* you can be confident that you've found your way to a method that can help you. Most marital conflict is solvable with effort and good humor. You're becoming more aware of your issues, and you're on the right path to restoring your marriage to health.

If you're thinking, *Uh oh! Things are worse than I thought they were! . . .* don't lose hope! Being in the midst of intense marital conflict can feel overwhelming, lonely, and like you should just quit now while you're ahead (err, behind). I believe in your ability to learn and grow and change together. Keep going and stick with the work.

DESCRIBE YOUR MARRIAGE VISION

Using your answers from the exercises in this chapter, describe your marriage vision and share your visions with each other.

The values that will define my marriage are _____

_____

_____ .

I understand that the issues that cause conflict for me, like _____

_____

_____ ,

consist of solvable and unsolvable parts.

I understand that my partner sees our marriage conflicts differently, like

_____

_____ .

I commit to building upon our relationship strengths, like _____

_____

_____ .

I will rid our marriage of poisons like _____

_____

_____ .

I will define our marriage by relationship cures like _____

_____

_____ .

Overall, I envision a marriage that is _____

_____

_____ .

I am willing to do _____

_____

_____

to make my vision of a marriage real.

Look back over the discussions and exercises in this chapter. What did you learn? What are the important new ideas for you? How will you use them to strengthen your marriage?

_____

_____

_____

_____

How are you feeling? How is your partner feeling? What are the similarities and differences in how you're feeling? (See appendix A for help with identifying your feelings.)

_____

_____

_____

_____

BENEATH THE SURFACE

The legacies of our families, our childhood experiences, and our past relationships can leave the bucket of our inner world with a hole in the bottom. The holes are from past traumas, learned shame, or fears. We look to our partners to fill up our bucket with water, to help us feel whole and soothed and full. But the water seeps out. So we ask for more water. And still, it seeps out.

The work of this chapter is to identify these holes and fix them through awareness and insight. With your bucket intact, the water you receive from your partner will satiate. But the work of this chapter is also to access your own source, to fill your own bucket with self-love and self-acceptance that flows from your own heart.

In other words, the work of this chapter is an opportunity to explore your past. It is a way of taking responsibility for yourself and acknowledging who you are based on who you have known. It's a chance to tell stories about what's happened to you. Some of these memories will be golden, and they'll warm your heart. Some will remind you of old emotional wounds, and you'll feel sad or angry.

Whatever feelings this work brings up for you, the emotional information will be helpful and meaningful. You must be willing to challenge yourself to grow and gain insight as an individual before you can work together with your partner to solve marriage conflicts. Remember, if you find you need more space to write than what is provided here, use a journal to further process your thoughts and feelings.

You may not feel ready to do anything with the deeply personal information you learn here. If you do feel comfortable sharing, you'll find discussion questions to guide a conversation with your partner. You may complete this chapter with more questions than answers. If that's the case, I recommend seeking a therapist to help you examine these questions. Even just a few sessions can be illuminating and healing. You don't have to do this work alone.

Family of Origin

From the moment we're born—and some might say even in utero—one of the primary ways we learn and grow is by absorbing information from the people around us. Our families of origin, the people who raised us and helped us understand the world, formed the context and environment that, in the most fundamental ways, shapes who we become. Within our families, we learn what is acceptable and unacceptable. We learn how to talk and how to think. We learn how to act when we're angry and what to do when we're sad. We learn how to celebrate achievements. We learn how to grieve.

As partners in a marriage, we often repeat the behaviors we witnessed among family members in our childhood, even those behaviors we tried to expunge. And we often, consciously or subconsciously, yearn for our partner to heal our childhood wounds.

The exercises in this chapter will help you examine your family of origin, especially through any unresolved childhood issues and the influences of your parents' marriage. First, let's get you thinking about your family through a child's imaginative eye.

DRAW YOUR FAMILY "AQUARIUM"

In the illustration on the next page, draw different sea creatures to represent each family member. Be creative! Use color! Pay attention to character traits, relative positions in the space, and size. Was your mom an amazing multitasker? Maybe she is an octopus with eight arms reaching in all directions. Was your little brother shy and withdrawn? Maybe he is a snail in a shell. Were your parents

preoccupied with work and your siblings? Maybe your animal is small, alone in the corner of the tank, looking at the rest of the creatures.

UNRESOLVED CHILDHOOD ISSUES

For most of us, the first memories that come to mind about our childhoods are images of family vacations, recess games, and the neighborhood we grew up in. But for some of us, these happy memories are punctuated by more painful ones— for example, witnessing our parents arguing, being teased on the playground, or sensing danger inside or outside our homes. Often, we see our childhood in our mind's eye as if we were watching home videos. Close your eyes for a few moments and let the images of your childhood come back to you.

CHART YOUR CHILDHOOD EXPERIENCES

List the childhood experiences you remember with the most emotion in the worksheet.

Positive Childhood Experience

_____

_____

_____

_____

How I Felt*

_____

_____

_____

_____

Negative Childhood Experience

_____

_____

_____

_____

How I Felt*

_____

_____

_____

_____

*See appendix A for help with identifying your feelings.

Positive Childhood Experience

_____

_____

_____

_____

_____

How I Felt*

_____

_____

_____

_____

_____

Negative Childhood Experience

_____

_____

_____

_____

_____

How I Felt*

_____

_____

_____

_____

_____

*See appendix A for help with identifying your feelings.

Positive Childhood Experience

_____
_____
_____
_____
_____

How I Felt*

_____
_____
_____
_____
_____

Negative Childhood Experience

_____
_____
_____
_____
_____

How I Felt*

_____
_____
_____
_____
_____

*See appendix A for help with identifying your feelings.

EXPLORE CHILDHOOD EXPERIENCES AND EFFECTS

Answer the following questions to explore the connections between the childhood experiences and emotions you identified in the previous exercise and the ways you're feeling in your marriage now.

To help you get started, here are Josh's and Linda's musings about the links between painful childhood experiences and their marriages now:

Josh remembers moving to a new neighborhood in the middle of fourth grade. "I was so angry at my parents for taking me away from my friends. I think it was the first time I remember feeling powerless over something that was happening to me." When he thinks about how he's been acting in his marriage to Heather, he sees a parallel. "Because I travel so much for work, I've been away from the kids many nights. When I'm home to help with bedtime, I feel wholly inadequate to be of much help. It's a similar feeling of powerlessness—and I take my frustration out on Heather."

Linda remembers sitting at the top of the stairs, listening to her parents enjoy a dinner party with friends. "I didn't feel left out, but I knew I wasn't welcome. I guess I felt longing." She didn't want her own kids to feel excluded like she did, so dinner parties with Tim and their friends always included the kids. "Maybe years of very little couple time—time for just us as adults—contributes to our feeling of disconnection now. The kids are grown and gone. Dinners are so quiet."

Are you seeking the positive feelings of your childhood in your marriage now?

_____

_____

_____

_____

Are you avoiding the negative feelings of your childhood in your marriage now?

_____

_____

_____

_____

How do your early childhood experiences influence the ways you act as a partner?

_____

_____

_____

_____

How do they contribute to how you feel about your marriage?

_____

_____

_____

_____

UNCOVERING EMOTIONAL WOUNDS AND FEARS

Now we're going to dig deeper, looking further underneath your childhood experiences of joy and frustration to uncover emotional wounds and fears you may still be carrying with you. You may find yourself starting to resist the work of this section—and that's okay. Take a break from it now and commit to picking it up again when you're ready.

It's not uncommon for us as children to feel afraid sometimes. But worse than fearing a monster under the bed, we feared what would happen because of the way our families treated us.

Circle the fears that you felt as a child or teenager or write in your own.
Then circle the ways you reacted in response to those fears.

Fears	Reactions
Of disappointing others	*Conformed*
Disapproved of	*Rebelled*
Excluded	*Lied/hid truths*
Forgotten	*Withdrew*
Invisible	*Tried to please*
Made to feel different	*Perfectionism*
Neglected/Ignored	*Escaped*
Never _____ enough	*Acted out*
Never _____ enough	*Sought attention*
Never _____ enough	*Sought love elsewhere*
Smothered	*Became clingy*
Unloved	*Acted in conventional/*
	traditional ways

Answer the open-ended questions below to help you make connections between your childhood wounds and the painful dynamics of your marriage now. Here are Beth's and Carlos's answers to help you get started:

Beth circled Forgotten *and* Rebelled. *"After my parents divorced, my dad was consumed by his new girlfriend. But after I'd get in trouble with my friends—staying out past curfew or drinking at a party—I'd have his full attention. I guess I made sure he wouldn't forget about me."* And she wonders, *"Do I act out in my life now so that Mei-Lin pays attention to me?"*

Carlos circled Never good enough *and* Tried to please. *"My older sibling was the perfect one, and my younger sibling was the baby. I was never as smart or accomplished as my older sibling, the perfect one, and I never got away with things like the sweet baby who could do no wrong. I think I spent most of my school years trying to make my parents happy, to make them notice the good things I was doing. And I think I try really hard to make Janelle happy now, too, but I want credit for it. That drives her crazy."*

Have you ever felt similar fears in your marriage?

_____

_____

_____

_____

Do you react to them in similar ways?

_____

_____

_____

_____

How does this compare to your feelings and responses to your partner when your needs for connection aren't being met?

_____

_____

_____

_____

How does your partner respond when you react in these ways?

_____

_____

_____

_____

How do you wish your partner would behave differently so that your childhood wounds would be healed?

_____

_____

_____

_____

YOUR PARENTS' MARRIAGE

Your parents' marriage was probably the first example you saw of what partnership between two adults looks like. The legacy of how they treated each other, what you witnessed between them in terms of affection and conflict resolution, ripples through your own marriage in subtle and not-so-subtle ways. In the following exercises, we'll explore what your relationship has inherited from your parents—whether or not they stayed together.

ASSESS YOUR PARENTS' MARRIAGE

In the worksheet, circle the answer for each statement that best represents your parents' marriage.

My parents compromised on making decisions.	Yes! Agree.	Not sure. Decisions were rarely made.	Disagree. One of them decided.
My parents were a united front and backed each other up.	Yes! Agree.	Not sure. Rules were always changing.	Disagree. They undermined each other.
My parents shared leadership in our family.	Yes! Agree.	Not sure. They fought a lot.	Disagree. One of them was the clear leader.
My parents spent time together just the two of them.	Yes! Agree.	Not sure. They usually spent free time apart.	Disagree. They didn't get along.
My parents were affectionate and loving in front of others.	Yes! Agree.	Not sure. They were private people.	Disagree. They were more like business associates.
My parents made the quality of their marriage a priority.	Yes! Agree.	Not sure. They seemed pretty independent.	Disagree. They endured negativity.

EXPLORE PATTERNS IN YOUR MARRIAGE

Answer the open-ended questions to help you make connections between the patterns in your parents' marriage and your own.

Here is Mei-Lin's response, to help you get started:

When Mei-Lin thinks about her parents' marriage, words like "reserved" and "stable" come to mind. She rarely witnessed them arguing, although they didn't seem to seek out each other's company either. She can't remember ever seeing them kiss or hug. Mei-Lin swore to herself she wouldn't settle for a passionless marriage like her parents'—that she would find a partner who loved her out loud. "I guess I got what I wished for—Beth and I have passion all right, but these days it's a heatedness that turns into arguments more often than it turns into sex."

Are you repeating patterns in your marriage that are similar to your parents' patterns?

_____

_____

_____

_____

What are some of the ways that you act like your mother?

_____

_____

_____

_____

What are some of the ways that you act like your father?

_____

_____

_____

_____

Thinking about yourself as a partner in your marriage, how are you different from your parents as partners? How are you similar?

_____

_____

_____

_____

If your parents divorced, do you know why? What was your experience of their marriage before the divorce and afterward? How does your experience of their divorce influence your marriage today?

_____

_____

_____

_____

_____

If your parents stayed together, do you know why? Were you ever worried that they would divorce, or, conversely, did you wish that they would?

_____

_____

_____

_____

_____

_____

_____

Previous Romantic Relationships

No experience is ever wasted. Thinking critically about our past romantic relationships can reveal helpful insights into our evolution as a partner. After our families of origin taught us the "rules" about love and marriage, we "practiced" them with our first partners. For this section, you may want to choose one past relationship in particular to explore or compile thoughts about your previous partners more generally.

The following exercises will help you examine your previous romantic relationships by learning about their successes and failures and how you may be repeating your past in your married present.

Check the successes and failures that occurred in your past relationship. Use the lines to fill in any you want to add.

Successes

☐ We had fun together.
☐ We shared a community of friends.
☐ We balanced time together and time apart.
☐ We trusted each other.
☐ The sex was great.

_____

_____

_____

_____

Failures

☐ One or both of us cheated.
☐ We didn't share the same values.
☐ One or both of us wasn't ready to grow up.
☐ We didn't put in the effort to solve our problems.
☐ One or both of us made other things a higher priority than the relationship.

_____

_____

_____

_____

What role did you play in the successes and failures of your past romantic relationships?

_____

_____

_____

_____

What automatic reactions did you learn that you're still working on now?

_____

_____

_____

_____

What decisions did you make about the kind of future partner you would seek?

_____

_____

_____

_____

What truths about love and partnership did you learn the hard way?

_____

_____

_____

_____

REPEATING THE PAST

One way to think about your marital conflict now is that it is made up of bad habits from your past. We start reacting to our partner's behaviors without thinking the situation through—sometimes, those automatic reactions can be traced back to previous romantic relationships.

HEATHER SAYS: *"One time, I was waiting for Josh to meet me at a coffee shop, but he was running late (he's still always late!), and he hadn't texted or called. When he finally walked in the door like no big deal, I felt frustrated and disrespected. I was so immediately angry that I wasn't even curious about what might have happened and didn't ask him if he was okay. I realized later that my previous boyfriend, Bryan, had primed me to be super sensitive to lateness— Bryan wasn't just late because he was forgetful or busy with school, he was late because he was playing some video game with his friends. Even though Josh isn't late for the same reasons, I still react like I used to with Bryan. Like he doesn't care enough about me to show up on time."*

HAVE I FELT THIS WAY BEFORE?

In what ways have your previous relationships primed you for what you are feeling now in your marriage?

_____

_____

_____

_____

Are you sensitive or, conversely, relaxed in response to the types of things that occurred in your past?

_____

_____

_____

_____

WHAT WOULD YOUR PAST PARTNER SAY?

Imagine that a past partner could watch a movie of your marriage now. What would they say about what's happening and about how you're behaving? Would they recognize your behaviors from your past relationship, or do you behave differently now?

_____

_____

_____

_____

WRITE A LETTER TO A FORMER PARTNER

Even though the lessons of past relationships are still with you and may be influencing how you act in or what you expect from your marriage now, it may be time to let your previous partner go. Perhaps you're still pining for a past partner or holding resentment toward them. The emotional energy of that relationship shouldn't cloud your marriage.

So as my mom told me when I was mourning a college boyfriend, "Put him on the bus." The metaphor means: Have a good last hug and say goodbye at the bus station, wave as the person boards (and maybe shed a tear), and let the bus drive away into the sunset.

Dear _____,

We met when I was _____ and you were

_____. Our relationship was characterized by

_____ and _____.

People said we'd _____. Even though

_____ happened in the end, our relationship

was not a waste. Because of you, I learned _____

about relationships. Because of you, I learned _____

about commitment. And because of you, I learned _____

about myself. I'll always remember how you used to tell me _____

_____.

I wish _____ for you in your life now. I hope

you _____ . Thank you for _____

_____ .

With gratitude and peace,

_____

Our History

"What was your relationship like in the beginning?" This is a question I ask couples in my practice, whether they've been fighting for years or only just had their first fight recently. I'm encouraged when I hear some version of "It was wonderful! We got along great—there was little fighting, good sex, and lots of fun." A passionate courtship that leads to happy newlywed days definitely gives marriage a positive start.

But sometimes the answer is something like "The seeds of our problems now were present at the beginning. Even then, we took each other for granted, sex lost its spark, and we got busier and busier." Although this answer suggests deep-rooted conflicts, the fact that the couple is ready now to address and resolve their relationship issues sets them on the path for a more stable and satisfying marriage for years to come.

The exercises in this section will help you remember the early days of your relationship to highlight not only the ways your marriage was built on positivity and connectedness but also the ways your compatibility sometimes manifests as conflict.

ORIGINAL ATTRACTION AND FALLING IN LOVE

Whether you knew each other as colleagues or friends before the spark of love took hold, or whether you were immediately and passionately inseparable, the original attraction you felt for each other was probably strong. Let's spend some time reminiscing about the rosy days of falling in love.

LOOK AT YOUR PHOTOS

Pictures are worth a thousand words. Open the photo album that holds pictures from your first months together. In your mind, answer the following questions as you look through them. What is the first picture taken of you together? Where are you? What are you doing? How do you remember feeling? What are your favorite pictures from your time dating? Why? Where are you? What are you doing? How do you remember feeling?

Do your cheeks hurt from smiling as you looked at those photos? I hope so! Bask in that warm, loving feeling for a few moments longer. Let it soak in and fill you up.

IDENTIFY ATTRACTION AND HIGHLIGHTS

Why did *this* partner at *that* time in your life make sense for you?

_____

_____

_____

_____

What attracted you to your partner?

_____

_____

_____

_____

Why was this attraction stronger than others?

_____

_____

_____

_____

What were the highlights of your first few months together?

_____

_____

_____

_____

EXPLORE SEEDS OF CONFLICT

Not everything may have been rosy. Think back to your early dating relationship and look for clues that were the seeds of the conflicts you're experiencing now. Write about these clues.

Here are Janelle's and Tim's answers to help you get started:

JANELLE SAYS: "*Our first big fight was over who was going to pay for dinner—we were both insisting on paying for the whole thing, and it got out of hand. When we were first dating, my parents were still depositing an allowance into my checking account. I guess I felt like it was no big deal for me to just pay for the whole thing. But for Carlos, he was coming from this place of 'I work hard for my money.' He explained later that being able to pay for things was a way of showing me how important I was to him. I should have realized then that money was going to be a big problem for us. We just approach it so differently.*"

TIM SAYS: "*On our first date, Linda just talked and talked about herself—where she'd traveled, her work-study job, her hobbies, and her close relationship to her mother. I remember being really interested and engaged with what she was saying. I liked the stories she told, and she made me laugh. But maybe that was a clue that she's a little self-centered. Something we've fought about almost our whole marriage is how even if she asked about my day at work, she was so wrapped up in the kids and her own busy day that she never really listened to my answer.*"

_____

_____

_____

_____

EARLY MARRIAGE YEARS

At some point along the way, you decided to get married. You chose a life together. You merged your families of origin into a new family. You merged your individual futures into a shared future. So now let's focus on your newlywed years, starting with the vows you made the day you were married.

REVISIT YOUR WEDDING

Whether you got married in a courthouse or a ballroom, whether you had an elaborate ceremony steeped in ritual or a short ceremony with traditional vows, call to mind your memories of your wedding ceremony. What do you remember fondly about your wedding day? What were the ideals of marriage that defined the start of your union? What promises did you make to your partner? Copy or paraphrase your vows here:

_____

_____

_____

_____

Take turns reading your vows aloud to your partner, then share your answers to the following discussion questions with each other: How do you feel, saying these important words again? How do you feel, hearing your partner's promises? How have each of you been doing, abiding by the promises you made on your wedding day?

_____

_____

_____

_____

MARRIAGE EXPECTATIONS: PROS AND CONS

When you agreed to become a married couple, you may have had some expectations of how your partner would behave in the marriage. Our expectations for our marriages, which we all have, often come from the legacies of our parents' relationship or from our own previous relationships. We can become disappointed when our expectations are not met, but having expectations isn't necessarily a negative thing. Here are some common pros and cons:

PRO	CON
By holding your relationship to high standards, you strive for high-quality interactions.	By holding your relationship to high standards, you are more likely to be disappointed.
Expecting good things becomes a self-fulfilling prophecy.	Expecting not-so-good things becomes a self-fulfilling prophecy.
High expectations of your partner's behavior leads you to be your best self, too.	Low expectations of your partner's behavior leads you to let yourself off the hook, too.

The key to managing expectations, whether high or low, is to be able to clearly articulate them to yourself and to your partner. This way, each of you has the chance to confront them, achieve them, or challenge them.

EXPLORE MARRIAGE EXPECTATIONS

What are your expectations in your marriage?

_____

_____

_____

_____

Where did those expectations come from; where did you learn to expect those things?

_____

_____

_____

_____

Do you think high expectations are a pro or a con for your marriage? What about low expectations?

_____

_____

_____

_____

IDENTIFY COMPLEMENTARY TRAITS

Often, the complementary traits that attract us to our partners in the beginning—the ones that are opposite our own styles—are the very ones we can't stand now. Couples in counseling with me usually balk at that word *complementary*. (Synonyms include *balancing, harmonizing,* and *paired.*) Being different from your partner certainly doesn't always feel positive.

Mark on the scales below where you and your partner fall on common complementary traits, or use the lines to write in your own.

Detail oriented	— — — — — — — — —	Big picture oriented
Emotional	— — — — — — — — —	Rational
Independent	— — — — — — — — —	Social
Introverted	— — — — — — — — —	Extroverted
Neat	— — — — — — — — —	Messy
Optimistic	— — — — — — — — —	Cynical
Relaxed	— — — — — — — — —	Anxious
Sarcastic	— — — — — — — — —	Earnest
Spontaneous	— — — — — — — — —	Calculating
_____	— — — — — — — — —	_____
_____	— — — — — — — — —	_____
_____	— — — — — — — — —	_____

For as many of these as you can, think back to when the differences between you brought you closer, rather than contributed to conflict. What was different then? How did you think about your differences as strengths, rather than as flaws?

_____

_____

_____

_____

DRAW A MARRIAGE BRIDGE

In the space below, draw a bridge that spans from your married past to your married future. Start with your early married years, continue to where you are now, and proceed to the end of the bridge where you are headed.

You can use colors, symbols, and words to draw the different parts of your bridge, what is above and below it, what it is made of, and what obstacles are along the way. Then, draw yourself at the point where you are in your married journey so far. Again, you can use colors, symbols, and words to illustrate how you're feeling, what resources you have, and who is traveling with you. If you feel comfortable, show your bridge to your partner and share with them about what you have drawn.

Look back over the discussions and exercises in this chapter. What did you learn? What are the important new ideas for you? How will you use them to strengthen your marriage?

_____

_____

_____

_____

How are you feeling? How is your partner feeling? What are the similarities and differences in how you're feeling? (See appendix A for help with identifying your feelings.)

_____

_____

_____

_____

PART 2

THE EIGHT STEPS

I hope you and your partner are already feeling more grounded in your marriage. The work of part 2 is to build on top of that foundation a new structure of a marriage that is repaired and enriched, and aligned with your visions for the future. This part is focused on changing the relationship dynamics and emotional energy between you. It's focused on teaching you skills where you're struggling, while encouraging you to continue what you're already doing well, so that you discover new ways of living with each other in love and friendship.

Each of the Eight Steps contains new ideas for how to approach your marriage and interact with each other in healthy, positive ways. It's important to work through all the exercises in each chapter in order to create a stronger marriage, as each is designed to help draw out what you're currently doing that is sabotaging your efforts at connection and replace it with healthier interactions. Each of the Eight Steps includes numerous activities called "Action Items," which help you make the concepts real in your life. These activities are specific actions you can take, either separately or together with your partner, to apply and reinforce the ideas you're learning.

There is no expected time frame in which you should complete each step—go at the pace that feels right to you and your partner, slowing down when you need to dig deep. There is no rush, but there is also no need to stall. Keep momentum going through each step, build on the successes, and learn from how and where you stumble. To get started, create a road map for working through part 2. Review the assessment of your everyday issues (page 11) and choose strengths and conflicts to focus on within each step.

Step 1: Communicate Effectively

Strengths _____ and _____

Conflicts _____ and _____

Step 2: Face Finances

Strengths _____ and _____

Conflicts _____ and _____

Step 3: Explore Intimacy

Strengths _____ and _____

Conflicts _____ and _____

Step 4: Reunite as *We*

Strengths _____ and _____

Conflicts _____ and _____

Step 5: Build Trust

Strengths _____ and _____

Conflicts _____ and _____

Step 6: Revisit Family

Strengths _____ and _____

Conflicts _____ and _____

Step 7: Redefine Relationship Roles

Strengths _____ and _____

Conflicts _____ and _____

Step 8: Make the Commitment

Strengths _____ and _____

Conflicts _____ and _____

COMMUNICATE EFFECTIVELY

Communication is the key to unlocking understanding, intimacy, and connection between two people. It's also the key to success in the Eight Steps—you and your partner must be able to communicate to address the issues that cause conflict.

It's actually a really complicated thing, to communicate effectively. Information must be transmitted out of your mind and heart, across the space between you, and received into the mind and heart of another person. You must combine a vast array of tools to do the transmitting: words, punctuation, body language, voice tone and pitch, and facial expressions. There is a different array of tools to do the receiving: distraction or attention, beliefs and expectations, interpretation and understanding, and avoidance of argument or validation. And you have to take turns sharing and listening, which means switching back and forth between two entirely separate sets of skills.

Take a moment to fill in the areas of strength and conflict from your marriage that will guide your focus in this step.

Step 1: Communicate Effectively

Strengths _____ and _____

Conflicts _____ and _____

Common Problems of Communication

Let's start with all the ways communication breaks down, derails, or is ineffective. The following information is meant to help you think about your style of communication now—where you're getting stuck and where you're successful as a couple.

DESTRUCTIVE PATTERNS OF COMMUNICATION

These five common problematic patterns disrupt clear, productive conversation:

1 **Escalation:** Responding negatively back and forth in a way that amplifies that negativity (increased emotional intensity in comments; anger turns to contempt)

2 **Invalidation:** Dismissing or minimizing the thoughts, feelings, or character of the other person (subtle or direct; putting the other person down)

3 **Absolutes:** Using words like *always* and *never* (inviting argument and disagreement; blaming or criticizing)

4 **Negative Interpretations:** Believing that the motives of the other person are more negative than they really are (confirmation bias: tendency to pay attention to evidence that confirms what you already believe is true)

5 **Withdrawal and Avoidance:** Unwillingness to stay with or engage with important conversations

IDENTIFY DESTRUCTIVE PATTERNS

Read the following exchange from Carlos and Janelle, and then underline and label the destructive patterns of communication you find.

JANELLE: *We really need to clean the apartment today.*

CARLOS: *But you just cleaned a few days ago. It's fine.*

JANELLE: *How come you always tell me it's fine! Your crap is everywhere, you didn't clean up dinner dishes last night, and the bathrooms—*

CARLOS: *Hang on. I did do the dishes last night, just not the pots. I didn't say I wouldn't help you today. I just don't think it's so bad around here.*

JANELLE: *This drives me crazy! I can't be the only one who cares about our home!*

CARLOS: *Really? You're telling me I don't care about our home? I help you ALL THE TIME! Wait. What are you doing?*

JANELLE: *Washing the pots, idiot. Clearly you're not going to do it.*

CARLOS: *Stop, come on, stop. I said I'd help.*

JANELLE: *Mmhm.*

CARLOS: *Fine! You never even gave me the chance. You do it. I don't care.*

JANELLE: *Right. Like I said.*

You probably noticed several destructive patterns, including escalation, absolutes, and withdrawal, to name a few. If you didn't identify all of them, don't worry! Keep working through the information in this chapter to understand what went wrong in this conversation.

FILTERS IN COMMUNICATION

Filters change what we hear, what we say, and how we interpret. These are some of the common forms:

1 **Distractions:** Factors in the environment that affect your ability to pay attention and focus (for example, street noise, thinking about something else, bad phone connection)
2 **Emotional states:** Mood (for example, bad moods or stress lead to negative interpretations and negative responses)
3 **Beliefs and expectations:** How you think about and what you expect from the person (for example, assumptions about where the other person is coming from, beliefs about the person from the past)

4 **Differences in style:** The script you carry in your mind about what is appropriate, relevant, meaningful (for example, culture, gender, past experiences, childhood modeling)

5 **Self-protection:** A response to anticipated rejection or pain (for example, amplifying what you say in preemptive attack or saying nothing at all to avoid conflict)

IDENTIFY YOUR FILTERS AND DISTORTED THINKING

Review the preceding lists and circle three filters and three types of distorted thinking (see page 64) that you recognize in yourself, and describe examples of how these play out in conversation with your partner.

_____

_____

_____

_____

From Agreement to Alignment

Effective communication in a marriage transmits important emotional information, solves problems, and bridges connection. It's not about right versus wrong. You've seen the bumper sticker: "You can be right or you can be married." Being right is about being in control, about winning the upper hand. Being wrong feels like losing, and often you experience internal conflict because, inside, you don't really agree that you are wrong.

But here's the thing—you can't control your partner's thoughts or how they feel! You can't control what they do! In a happy marriage, we must let go of our need to control our partner and accept them for who they are. We need to find ways to compromise by blending our different perspectives into a common understanding.

DISTORTED THINKING

These 10 examples of distorted thinking can also wreak havoc on communication because they convince us that what we're thinking is true and accurate without all the facts:

1   **Mind reading:** assuming you know what the other is thinking without evidence

2   **Fortune telling:** anticipating that things will turn out badly, that your prediction is an already-established fact

3   **Catastrophizing:** thinking that what has happened or what will happen is so awful that you won't be able to cope

4   **Overgeneralizing:** perceiving a global pattern of negatives on the basis of a single event

5   **Dichotomous thinking:** viewing events or people in all-or-nothing terms

6   **Disqualifying the positive:** rejecting positive experiences or thoughts by insisting they "don't count," thereby maintaining a negative outlook contradicted by day-to-day experiences and thoughts

7   **Emotional reasoning:** assuming that feelings reflect the way things are

8   **"Should statements":** behaving or making decisions motivated by "should" or "should not" beliefs

9   **Personalization:** accepting responsibility for a negative external event that is not personal

10 **Regret orientation:** focusing on the idea that you made a mistake in the past rather than on how you could be better in the present

So instead of communication with the aim of agreement, let your aim be alignment. Let it be about attunement, partnering with each other as a team. You don't have to agree. You don't have to become a clone of your partner and see things the same way. But you do have to be able to communicate what is in your head and heart, and listen to what is in your partner's head and heart. You need to be able to tune in to your partner to solve problems together, make decisions together, and get along.

When you're aligned, *both* of you are able to walk away from a conversation saying to yourselves, "I know that my partner understands what I said and how I feel." (Which means, since your partner is saying the same thing as they are walking away, that you were able to communicate your understanding of their ideas and feelings.) You do this through two fundamental communication skills: assertiveness and validation.

ASSERTIVENESS

I want your stance as a speaker and a listener to be assertive. To be assertive is to claim the middle space between your own experience and the experience of another. Assertiveness is the stance that allows for mutual cooperation without it being at the expense of oneself or the self of your partner. The following table helps you identify the qualities associated with three types of stances, with assertiveness as the happy medium.

| | | STANCE | |
	Passive	Assertive	Aggressive
As Sender of Communication	Self-denying	Self-enhancing	Self-enhancing at expense of others
	Inhibited	Expressive	Explosive
	Makes passive statements (abdicate your experience)	Makes "I statements" (declare your experience)	Makes blaming statements (deflect your experience)
	Feels hurt and anxious	Feels good about self, confident	Feels anger and righteousness
	Allows others to choose	Chooses for self	Chooses for others
	Does not achieve desired goal (avoidance)	May achieve desired goal through cooperation	Achieves desired goal through force

continued

	STANCE		
	Passive	**Assertive**	**Aggressive**
As Receiver of Communication	Feels guilt, shame, confusion	Maintains self-esteem and sense of worth	Activates defensiveness
	Activates self-deprecation	Encourages expression and dialogue	Triggers counterattack and escalation
	Does not achieve desired goal (unknowing)	May achieve desired goal through cooperation	Pushes back to prevent desired goal

ASSERTIVE SPEAKING FROM YOUR HEART

Speaking assertively from your heart is how you keep your message both valuable and valued. Usually, it's our heads that do the talking, the part of us that is reactive, seeks agreement, and seeks to convince or prove. Your heart is the part of you that is receptive, seeks alignment with your partner, and seeks to love and be loved. Speak from that part. Here are two tips for how to assertively speak from your heart and an exercise to practice each one:

1 **Communicate the softer side of your emotions**. When we speak from anger or frustration, our partner's alarm bells can go off. But anger is often a secondary emotion, and the primary one is usually more tender and more difficult to say—emotions like sadness, disappointment, fear, regret, embarrassment, and hurt.

HEATHER SAYS: *"The other day, Josh was driving all of us to dinner with friends, and as we approached an intersection, he wasn't slowing down enough. I thought he was going to run the red light, so I yelled at him, 'STOP, you idiot!' He slammed on the brakes and yelled back at me, 'JEEZ! I'm qualified to drive, Heather!' I know I came across so angry—he was sufficiently taken aback by my anger that he got defensive—but really what I was feeling was fear. I was afraid we'd get in an accident."*

Think about a time recently when you felt angry or frustrated with your partner. Think now about the softer side of your emotions that the anger covered up. What were they? (See appendix A for help with identifying your feelings.)

_____

_____

_____

_____

2   **Use "I Statements."** Speaking from your own perspective is an essential part of assertiveness and of speaking from your heart. Start sentences with "I" and then follow with a verb: "I think" or "I believe" or "I wish." But be careful with "I feel." Sentences that start with "I feel" must remain a strong signal to your partner that important emotional information is about to come next: *I feel sad, I feel overwhelmed, I feel misunderstood.* We often use the phrase "I feel" to soften a thought or opinion by putting *like* after it. "I feel like you . . ." Instead, use phrases like "It seems to me" or "I would prefer that" to soften a thought or opinion.

JOSH'S HEAD SPEAKING: *"I feel like you don't care about my day, Heather. You didn't even ask me about my meeting this morning. So, no, I'm not interested in telling you what I'm thinking about or how my day was. Next time, I just won't tell you about work so I don't get so disappointed when you don't follow up."*

JOSH'S HEART SPEAKING: *"I feel hurt and confused, Heather. When we talked yesterday, I told you about my meeting this morning, but then you didn't ask me about it specifically over dinner. So then I started to withdraw from you. Next time, instead of asking, 'How was your day?' more generally, could you ask me specifically about what you knew was going on for me at work?"*

Fill in the blanks in the prompt for heart speaking:

I feel _____ (a feeling word!) when
_____(describe the situation neutrally,
nonblamingly, nonjudgmentally). So then I _____
(your reaction, what you do next based on your feeling in the situation). Next time,
_____ (your request for a different future feeling/
situation/reaction).

ASSERTIVE LISTENING WITH YOUR HEART

Listening assertively from your heart is how you maintain your own perspective while helping your partner feel heard. Again, when our heads do the listening, we drift into debate, argument, right versus wrong, what is *True* with a capital *T*. But when we allow our hearts to do the listening, we are seeking to understand rather than judge, to suspend our reality to consider another person's reality. And not just any other person's reality—that of our partner in marriage.

Then, after you listen, you need to speak. This is the work of validation, to communicate back to your partner what you heard them say. Just repeating it back isn't enough. You're not meant to be a parrot! You're meant to be a person who—even if you experienced the situation differently or feel differently or think differently (of course you do, you're a different person!)—can understand what your partner sees, feels, and thinks. And you should be able to communicate that understanding back to your partner.

But wait! I hear you shout. *If I tell my partner that I understand, then I'm agreeing with them!*

You're not after agreement here; you're after alignment. It's possible to disagree *and* validate. It's possible to have experienced something differently or interpreted something differently *and* to communicate an understanding of how your partner experienced that same thing and interpreted that same thing.

Here are two tips for how to assertively listen from your heart, and an exercise to practice each one:

1 **Pay attention through mindfulness.** Mindfulness is helpful no matter what type of therapy my clients are seeking. That's because learning how to harness the power of mindfulness and feeling its benefits in your relationships is a great way to start experiencing positive results from therapy.

One of my favorite ways to teach mindfulness is through a well-known quote by Jon Kabat-Zinn: *"Mindfulness means paying attention in a particular way: on purpose, in the present moment, and non-judgmentally."*

Let's break that quote down to really understand what he's saying:

Mindfulness means paying attention . . .

Mindfulness requires us to turn off the autopilot that is so often in control of our thoughts and actions. And, let's face it, sometimes autopilot is helpful! Routine and muscle memory may make task completion quicker and easier, but when we're setting out to be mindful, paying attention is key. It requires focus and consideration.

in a particular way: on purpose, . . .

Kabat-Zinn builds on the idea of attention by pointing us to *intention*. You're practicing mindfulness on purpose because you want to, because it's important to stay focused on the information coming from your partner so you can fully absorb it. Paying attention with intention is how your partner feels heard after sharing and how you're able to reflect the fullness of what they shared. Doing something on purpose gives it meaning and importance.

in the present moment . . .

Mindfulness is synonymous with the present. When we're being mindful, we resist the urge to time-travel in our minds, either to the past down memory lane or into the future of worry and what-ifs. Train your brain to quiet its own thoughts and learn to ignore distractions. When you're paying attention, you're not interrupting, you're not preparing your rebuttal, and you're not thinking about what you want to eat for dinner.

and non-judgmentally.

At the end of the quote, Kabat-Zinn reminds us that our orientation to mindfulness is important, too. For some of us, being nonjudgmental may be the hardest part about it. We must shift our thinking from judgment about what we're hearing (labeling, opinions, preferences), to curiosity (What do I notice? How do I feel?), and finally to compassion (empathy, tolerance, acceptance, kindness). There is no right or wrong way; there is no success or failure. There is only listening to your partner in the present moment, just as they are, without changing what you hear.

NOTICE HOW YOUR MIND WANDERS

Does your mind wander when listening to your partner? Where does it go? How does it feel when you notice your partner's attention is not on you when you are speaking?

_____

_____

_____

_____

2 **Listen for what's underneath.** When you're having trouble wrapping your head around what your partner is saying, remember that by listening with your heart you are able to hear what is underneath their words or body language. Ask yourself what might be motivating them to act this way, say these things, and believe this reality.

MEI-LIN SAYS: *"Beth often comes home late from being out with friends, after I'm already asleep. So one of our classic fights is when I ask her in the morning, 'How was last night?' And she says, 'Fine, I got home at one in the morning and had lots of fun.' And then I ask how she's feeling in the morning and she'll usually minimize it. 'Oh, I definitely had a few. But I feel totally fine this morning, I'm not hung over or anything.' Clearly, she has a headache!"*

So what's underneath Beth's answer? Why would she minimize how she feels in the morning? Maybe underneath her deflection is embarrassment or shame, or maybe avoidance of a conflict.

So instead of saying, "You're lying, Beth!," which would escalate the conversation and provoke more defensiveness from Beth, Mei-Lin challenges her in a different way: "Well, I know Kim was out with you last night, and she's a big drinker. I'm sure you felt swept up in the night, and I'm glad you had a good time. I just wish you'd feel comfortable talking about how you're really feeling this morning."

Instead of feeling attacked, Beth may be more likely to connect with Mei-Lin's concerns. Mei-Lin listened for feelings underneath and communicated Beth's experience from Beth's perspective.

PRACTICE LISTENING FOR WHAT'S UNDERNEATH

Think about a recent interaction with your partner that left you feeling confused or as if there was more to the story. What feelings can you identify that may have been underneath what your partner was saying?

_____

_____

_____

_____

How could you communicate your understanding of what's underneath to make it safe for your partner to share?

_____

_____

_____

_____

VALIDATION

Validation is a tricky word—couples in my office get hung up on it all the time. "If I validate what she said, I give it validity—legitimacy, rationality, truth. But what she's saying isn't true!" you tell me. "He's seeing it all wrong!" you shout.

Yes, according to *you*. But not according to your partner. I'm asking you to give up your goal of being right, of forcing agreement. Instead, focus your energy on the goal of being aligned, of moving together in the same direction.

Validation is how you communicate that you understand what you are hearing, that your partner's thoughts/feelings/actions make sense given their situation and perspective. And you *are* actually giving what your partner is saying validity; you're acknowledging that there is more than one way (your way) to think about a problem, feel about a situation, or believe about the future.

Validation reduces conflict intensity, is nonjudgmental, and is good for all relationships, not just marriage. Here's how you do it:

- Acknowledge what you hear by observing and describing nonjudgmentally. For example, "I can see that you're really upset about this" or "The way you see it, if we fly to my parents' house for Thanksgiving like we did last year, it'll seem to your parents that we're avoiding them."
- Accept what you hear without necessarily agreeing with or endorsing or liking what you hear. For example, "I hear that you are frustrated that I didn't call ahead of time that my meeting would run late," or "I understand that you are disappointed that my mom didn't make the trip for our baby shower."
- Use healthy, effective communication skills: Actively listen and pay attention (eye contact, body orientation, relaxed face); state feelings and nonverbal observations without judging (respond in a way that takes what is said seriously); and show tolerance and communicate understanding (especially if you do not approve of or agree with what is being expressed).

Rules of Engagement

When you are in the midst of a conflict with your partner, remember these simple rules of engagement: *Stop, Drop, Swap*. This is a trick for fighting fair that I teach couples in counseling. It's a shorthand way of remembering and simplifying the rules of engagement when you're in conflict with your partner and want to get the conversation back to a healthy place.

1 **Stop**—Stop what you're doing! Minimize distractions—put away the phones, turn off the TV, pay attention to your body language. Tune in to your feelings and triggers so that you understand your own emotional state.
2 **Drop**—Drop your agenda, your defenses, your judgments, and your assumptions so that you can participate with love and respect and remain curious about your partner's feelings and words and ideas, even if—especially if—they differ from your own.
3 **Swap**—Talk to each other with sensitive honesty; soften harsh truths you anticipate will be hard for your partner to hear without minimizing your own need to be open and honest. Use effective communication skills like an assertive stance, mindfulness, and validation.

And if things still spiral into miscommunication—take a break! (See step 5 for some guidelines on taking a time-out.)

PRACTICE "STOP, DROP, SWAP"

Over the next two days, commit yourself to practicing these simple rules of engagement: Stop, Drop, Swap. Then check in with yourself by asking the following questions:

What were the red flag moments that reminded you to STOP?

_____

_____

_____

_____

What self-soothing techniques did you use to DROP your own agenda and defenses?

_____

_____

_____

_____

How well did you practice the SWAP of information and feelings?

_____

_____

_____

_____

Active Listening

Active listening is the phrase our culture uses to name effective communication, but it's admittedly not the best name. After the couple in my office roll their eyes, they usually dismiss active listening as workplace community-building mumbo-jumbo, or they assume it's about parroting back what you heard. Communication "examples" go like this:

"I want to make a salad for dinner. I like salad better than pasta."

"I heard you say you want to eat salad for dinner because you like salad better than pasta."

Doesn't that fall flat? Active listening is so much more than repeating what you've heard. It requires two big parts—the speaker part and the listener part. I use the metaphor of passing a rock back and forth with every couple I counsel to illustrate what this process is really like.

You carefully select the rock you want to share. You spend some time studying it, deciding how you want to describe it. Then you hold it out to your partner. You say, "I have something to show you. This is my rock. Do you see how it is this color

THE PAUSE

Even though communication may be difficult right now, here's some really good news: Positive shifts in your thinking from seeking agreement to seeking alignment, and in your interactions with your partner, can all boil down to one small step. Here it is:

Pause.

Yep, that's it!

Just pausing for one moment opens you up to new possibilities for response, engagement, and choices. During the pause, you ask yourself questions like "What is my primary goal here?" and "What is a nondefensive way to show my partner I want to try again?" During the pause, you remind yourself about all the love and joy you're capable of, like "I believe in us and I know we can recover from this disagreement" and "You are worthy of my love, even when you make mistakes."

It's just one small step, but it's pretty radical. A pause is all it takes to break out of ineffective communication patterns and make a different, healthier choice toward loving each other, aligning with each other, and reconnecting with each other.

PRACTICE "THE PAUSE"

The next time a conversation starts to derail, practice taking just a moment to pause.

_____

_____

_____

_____

What's helpful for you in the pause? A deep breath? Counting to 10?

_____

_____

_____

_____

When the pause is over, how are you better able to refocus on healthy communication skills?

_____

_____

_____

_____

How did your partner respond to the pause?

_____

_____

_____

_____

and has this shape? It has these features, and it's bumpy here but smooth there. This is where I first collected this rock, and this is why I still have it. I must be careful with this part of the rock—it's sharp. This is how heavy it feels to me. This is how I feel about this rock. This is what it means to me."

Your partner is listening. They are paying close attention to what you are saying and how you are saying it. They are not interrupting you, challenging you, or dismissing you. They are absorbing the feelings behind your words. You hand the rock to your partner and they hold it.

They look down and say, "I see your rock. I see its color and its shape, and I understand the ways you described it. I see its features and how its texture changes. You found it there, and that is why you still hold on to it. I'm being careful with the sharp part. I can see why you must be careful with the sharp part. I understand how its weight is heavy for you. You have these feelings about the rock. This is what the rock means to you." Your partner has matched your tone and your emotions.

Your partner hands the rock back to you. It's the same rock you passed to them.

Things that didn't happen:

You didn't throw your rock at your partner. You didn't leave it lying around, hoping they'd stumble upon it. You didn't hand over more than one rock at a time. You didn't hand it over without a considered explanation. You didn't refuse to hand it over. You didn't grab it back.

Your partner didn't drop it or refuse to hold it. They didn't put it in their pocket and keep it for their own. They didn't take a chisel or paintbrush to it. They didn't mold it with one of their own rocks. They didn't argue about its color, its shape, or its weight. They didn't throw it back at you.

IDENTIFY YOUR "ROCKS"

Choose one of your recurring arguments from chapter 1, and one of your childhood experiences (positive or negative) from chapter 2. Use the following prompts to describe these "rocks," but don't share them yet with your partner.

Name the rock—what is it called?

_____

_____

_____

_____

Describe the rock's features—what are the important parts for you?

_____

_____

_____

_____

What does your partner need to know about it?

_____

_____

_____

_____

How does it feel to you? What does it mean to you?

_____

_____

_____

_____

Where did it come from?

_____

_____

_____

_____

PRACTICE ACTIVE LISTENING

It's time to practice the overall skill of effective communication. Remember, passing your rocks is a metaphor for how to express empathy, feel heard and understood, and avoid recurring arguments. Use the prompts in the previous exercise to craft what you want to share. Then take turns practicing as the speaker and the listener, both of you doing it from your *hearts*.

How did that go?

_____

_____

_____

_____

Where did you get stuck as the speaker?

_____

_____

_____

What was your experience of being the listener?

_____

_____

_____

_____

Look back over the discussions and exercises in this chapter. What did you learn? What are the important new ideas for you? How will you use them to strengthen your marriage?

_____

_____

_____

_____

How are you feeling? How is your partner feeling? What are the similarities and differences in how you're feeling? (See appendix A for help with identifying your feelings.)

_____

_____

_____

_____

ACTION ITEMS

Here are specific actions you can take to implement the lessons and ideas you learned in this chapter:

1 When watching a movie or TV show or reading a novel, be on the lookout for destructive patterns of communication. Hone your detective skills!

2 Aside from the "passing a rock" metaphor for active listening, try to think of a different image that illustrates what it's like to speak and listen from your heart.

3 Practice the communication skills in this step ("I statements," the pause, and Stop, Drop, Swap) in other areas of your life besides your marriage—for example, with colleagues, friends, children, and other family members.

4 Explore the power of mindfulness to quiet your mind through meditation, yoga, or communing with nature.

5 Heart speaking is an important skill when communicating with _ourselves_, too, just as much as it's important when communicating with our partner. Pay attention to your self-talk, and practice being gentler and kinder to yourself.

FACE FINANCES

Ah, money. Many of us disagree with our partners about money and don't know how to resolve our financial differences. Fortunately, my work with couples has shown me that disagreements over money can be successfully managed no matter how long you've been together. In this step, I'll help you uncover what money means to you and assess whether the way you and your partner have merged finances is healthy for your partnership.

To prepare for the work in this step, I recommend that you gather information about your finances: Print a recent credit card statement, and make a list of all of your accounts. Having concrete information about your unique financial situation will help you make the most of this step. I am not trained as a financial expert, and you should always consult with your trusted financial advisers, like an accountant or portfolio manager, before making changes to your marital financial decision making or account structures.

Take a moment to fill in the areas of strength and conflict from your everyday issues assessment (page 11), which will guide your focus in this step.

Step 2: Face Finances

Strengths _____ and _____

Conflicts _____ and _____

Money Attitudes

Money is something concrete—dollars and cents, debt-to-income ratios. It is also conceptual, symbolizing values, preferences, and emotions. The tricky thing about money is that the conceptual and the concrete mutually influence each other: The attitudes you hold about money change how you spend the dollars and, similarly, your financial situation contributes to how you feel from day to day.

Differences in money attitudes are usually at the root of financial conflict in a marriage. Do you want the luxury car instead of the base model because money represents status, because dollars communicate to others your value? Does your partner want the base model instead of the luxury car because money represents security, because dollars should be reserved for unexpected expenses? Without digging deeper to understand what money means to you, arguments about leather seats and moonroofs will end in misunderstanding and a decision that puts the needs and desires of one partner over those of the other.

ASSESS WHAT MONEY MEANS TO YOU

Assess your orientation to money. Thinking about money as an external representation of priorities, rank the following priorities, or write in your own, in order of importance to you when thinking about money:

_____ Comfort   _____

_____ Control   _____

_____ Entertainment   _____

_____ Generosity   _____

_____ Security   _____

_____ Status   _____

How do your attitudes about money influence your behavior with money?

_____

_____

_____

_____

How are your rankings different from your partner's?

_____

_____

_____

_____

Do these differences cause conflict between you?

_____

_____

_____

_____

MONEY GROWING UP

Often, our attitudes about money come from the ways we witnessed our parents handle money. Think back to your family growing up. How did your parents talk about money? What orientation to money do you have that you learned from your parents? Here are two common answers:

- **Scarcity Mind-set:** There was never enough money growing up, and even as a kid you knew it. The answer was _no_ to the newest gadget, and pleasure spending, like a vacation or going to the movies, was rare. _There will never be enough money._ Money is stressful. Money is something to be very careful with.
- **Magical Mind-set:** Sometimes there was a lot of money, and sometimes the budget was tight, but the kids never really knew either way. The answer was

yes to the newest gadget, even when debt was incurred to pay for it, and the same with pleasure spending. *There will always be enough money!* Like magic, money sorts itself out. Money isn't something to be careful with.

EXPLORE INHERITED ATTITUDES ABOUT MONEY

What money attitudes did you inherit from your parents?

_____

_____

_____

_____

How is your inherited mind-set about money the same as or different from your partner's?

_____

_____

_____

_____

MONEY IN YOUNG ADULTHOOD

Another developmental period that has lasting effects on attitudes about money is young adulthood. Think back to the time of your first job or career, or the first time you were handling the money you earned on your own. How did you make spending decisions? Did you learn the hard way about credit card debt?

WRITE YOUR FINANCIAL HISTORY STORY

Write the story of your financial history, paying attention to how your young adult experiences with money shaped how you view money now, and then compare your financial history story to your partner's. How is it similar or different?

Here is Tim's example, to help you get started:

TIM SAYS: *"My parents really instilled in me the value of working hard, and I've been working since I was a teenager, starting with odd jobs. I had a newspaper route, I stocked produce at our neighborhood market, and the summer I turned 17, I started helping on the construction site of a new hotel in our downtown. From a young age, if I wanted something, I had to pay for it myself. I was proud to—I took girlfriends to the movies with my own money, and I saved and saved and bought my first car. The more money I made, the more money I wanted, so I've always been willing to work more and longer. It's interesting to think now about retirement. What will I do with all that energy I've put into work?"*

Money as Power

Money is a way to wield influence. It can be used to exert power over another person, such as buying their loyalty, suppressing their freedom, or establishing who is in charge. Using money as power in this way is one of the most damaging dynamics in a marriage. When one partner has more power because they have more money, decision making becomes one-sided, and worth becomes tied to dollars.

HEATHER SAYS: *"Now that I'm not working, Josh and I fight way more often about money. Actually, it's more like now we use money as a weapon during our fights. The other night when we were arguing about whether Mason's private preschool was worth the monthly expense, Josh said something like, 'Well since I make all the money right now, I get to make the call on this one.' He never used to lord money over me like that; it really stung. Just because his work pays money doesn't give him the right to make all the decisions!"*

Money can also be used to exert power over a situation, such as throwing money at problems, changing your standard of living, or maintaining control over money to maintain independence. Using money as a tool to control or change your lifestyle can be positive or negative, so it's important to be thoughtful about the role money plays for you. For example, refusing to merge money with your partner as a way to maintain power over your money can undermine the spirit of partnership and trust that marriage requires.

EXPLORE MONEY AS POWER

Be honest with yourself—do you use money to exert power over your partner or over your situation, or do you experience your partner using money to exert power over you? Mark the extent to which you agree or disagree with each of the following statements, and then total your points:

Strongly Disagree = 1 point   Agree = 3 points

Disagree = 2 points   Strongly Agree = 4 points

1 The person who makes more money has the final say about how that money is spent. _____
2 I feel pressure to align with my partner's, or my partner's family's, more expensive lifestyle, even though it is a financial stretch for me to do so. _____
3 A partner must ask permission before spending money they didn't earn. _____
4 Picking up the entire dinner bill or buying lavish presents isn't simply a benevolent generosity—it's a way of establishing respect and influence. _____
5 Saving and investment decisions are made unilaterally to benefit each partner individually. _____

If you scored 13 to 20 points, you use money to exert influence over your partner and others. Dig deep into this chapter to examine the role of money in your partnership. Remain open and curious about new ideas and new strategies for dealing with money as a team.

If you scored 5 to 12 points, you do not use money as a way to exert influence over your partner and others. The exercises and ideas in this chapter will help you further explore how money flows between you as equals.

Compare scores with your partner and discuss. Do you feel differently about money as power?

_____

_____

_____

_____

ORGANIZE STATE OF THE UNION MEETINGS

A commitment to handle money productively as a couple shifts the power to your marriage instead of to either one of you. A State of the Union meeting is meant to help you take stock of your finances together so that you operate as a financial team. At the end of each meeting, you'll have an action plan for your money.

Once a quarter (four times a year), set aside an hour or two for a State of the Union meeting. During this meeting, you will review together the financial picture of the previous three months and look ahead to the next three. Ask and answer questions like:

- How did we do following our budget last quarter?
- What were the unexpected expenses?
- What should we do with the money we saved?
- What changes do we need to make to our budget in the next quarter?
- Are there big purchases coming up or bills that will be due?
- How healthy does our short-term financial future seem?

If the conversation starts to derail or emotions start to run high, flip back to step 1 and review the skills of effective communication.

SET SHARED FINANCIAL GOALS

No matter how your money is merged or budgeted, it's important to share financial goals as a married couple. Setting shared financial goals is another way for you and your partner to operate as a financial team. Write your goals separately, then share them with one another.

Short-Term Goals (6 months to 1 year):

1 _____

_____

_____

_____

2 _____

_____

_____

_____

3 _____

_____

_____

_____

Medium-Term Goals (1 to 4 years):

1 _____

_____

_____

_____

2 _____

_____

_____

_____

3 _____

_____

_____

_____

Long-Term Goals (5 to 10 years):

1 _____

_____

_____

2 _____

_____

_____

3 _____

_____

_____

THE VALUE OF UNPAID WORK

"We're a team working toward a common goal." I heard this phrase over and over growing up, and it's one I use with the couples I counsel as well. When you and your partner function as a team, *all* work is valued—not just the work that generates a paycheck. Other work done for the family is just as important!

Some of this work is task-based, like childcare, household chores, grocery shopping, or car maintenance. Other aspects of unpaid work require mental energy, like remembering extended family members' birthdays, anticipating when it's time to replenish pantry items, researching local sports leagues for kids, or knowing what to pack for the kids for vacation. Neither kind of labor, household or mental/emotional, should be thankless. (There's more on the complex aspect of gender roles and mental load in step 7.)

UNPAID WORK COMPARISON

List all of the unpaid work do you for your family, and then compare lists with your partner. If one list is longer than the other, notice how that makes you feel. Again, instead of slipping into resentment or defensiveness, revisit the skills in step 1 to share your feelings, concerns, and requests for change.

1 _____

2 _____

3 _____

4 _____

5 _____

6 _____

7 _____

8 _____

9 _____

10 _____

PAY ATTENTION TO UNPAID WORK

Over the next week, pay attention to when your partner does unpaid work for the family. Make an effort to notice and offer appreciation, either verbally or by leaving little thank-you notes for each other. Expressing gratitude is a meaningful way to show each other the value of teamwork in your marriage. What was your experience?

Merging Money

Another common underlying cause of fights about money is that the way couples have chosen to merge their money doesn't suit their couple style. Often, couples follow what they know, either repeating the way their parents merged money or following their friends' examples.

In my work with couples, I've come to use a "color of money" metaphor to illustrate how the money each partner earns either stays separate, as blue or red, or becomes joint as purple. There is no right way to merge money—each couple should make the decision based on their style and preferences. And whatever way you choose to do it, a high level of communication is needed!

Here are three basic structures for merging money, and an example from three of our couples:

TOTALLY SEPARATE

This structure is high on straightforwardness and low on trust. The way it works is simple—money always stays blue or red. Blue money pays blue expenses and saves for blue's retirement. Red money pays off red debt and buys red's happy hour drinks. There is no purple money. Each is responsible for their own spending and saving decisions, so trust isn't super important.

> Beth and Mei-Lin have no joint accounts together. Each woman's salary goes into her own checking account. Each buys her own groceries, her own clothes, and saves for her own retirement. Big shared expenses like the mortgage payment are split 50/50, and smaller shared expenses are divvied up somewhat equally (for example, Beth pays the vet bills and Mei-Lin pays for the cat food, grooming, toys, and treats).

SEPARATE AND TOGETHER

This structure is low on straightforwardness and medium on trust. The way it works is complex, because the possible mixtures and flows of blue or red or purple money are as unique as each couple. Blue money pays some blue expenses, and purple money pays for others. Red money could pay off red debt, or purple money could pay debt. In each scenario, the couple is responsible for determining the rules about which color money is for which kind of spending. To the extent that money is purple, trust is required.

Josh and Heather have both joint accounts and individual accounts, and their system is flexible as their income changes. For example, when both Josh and Heather were working, 80 percent of Josh's salary and 80 percent of Heather's salary were deposited into the joint account, leaving 20 percent of each for personal spending. Once Heather left her job to stay home with the kids, 100 percent of Josh's salary has gone into the joint account. If there is money left over at the end of the month, they split it 50/50 into their personal accounts.

TOTALLY TOGETHER

This structure is high on straightforwardness and high on trust. The way it works is also simple—money is always purple. Purple money pays blue expenses and saves for blue's retirement. Purple money pays off red debt and buys red's happy hour drinks. There is no distinction between red money and blue money. Spending and savings decisions are entirely joint, and a high level of trust is required.

Tim and Linda have always had only joint accounts. Whether the credit card charge was for their kids' camp registration, Linda's new dress, or an oil change for Tim's car, the money always came from the joint checking. And when Linda's mother died, leaving her a small inheritance, she and Tim opened a joint investment account with the money.

HOW MONEY FLOWS

Next, I'll help you visualize how your money flows to show where your income comes from and how it merges and divides so that you can assess what is and isn't working about your system.

Here is how Carlos and Janelle drew their money flow, and how they described what's working, as an example. Note the differences in the amounts of money and how the "dollars" combine and divide through the flow of accounts:

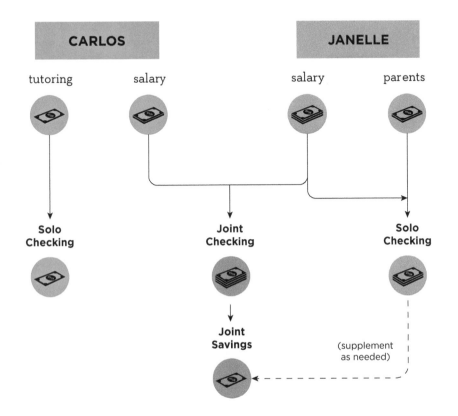

What's working for Carlos and Janelle:

- *"We have just enough money to pay joint expenses from our joint account."*
- *"Each of us has at least some personal spending money."*

What's not working for Carlos and Janelle:

- *"Our amounts of personal spending money aren't equal."*
- *"We're not saving as much as we want to."*

MONEY FLOW: PRE-DISCUSSION DRAWING

In the space provided, draw your money flow to show where your income comes from and how it merges and divides. Use the colors red, blue, and purple as described in the previous section and be clear about the differences in the amounts of money between accounts. Then describe what's working well and what's causing problems.

What's working for you and your partner?

_____

_____

_____

_____

What's not working for you and your partner?

_____

_____

_____

_____

Using the communication skills you learned in step 1, discuss your answers to the following questions and take conversation notes:

Does the flow match your priorities and marriage values?

_____

_____

_____

_____

Does it reflect your partnership structure's place on the spectrum of traditional to equitable?

_____

_____

_____

_____

How would you want to change the flow to suit your styles better?

_____

_____

_____

_____

Here is how Carlos and Janelle discussed making shifts in how money flows through their accounts. (Notice how they're practicing the skills of active listening!):

CARLOS: *I feel conflicted about getting money from your parents. On one hand, I consider that totally your money and don't want to claim it. On the other hand, we could put it to use for joint expenses and that would free up our salaries for other spending. I just don't want it to seem like I'm benefiting from money that isn't mine.*

JANELLE: *I understand how you feel conflicted and that although you see how we could use the money together, it's important to you that the money from my family stay "in my family." Did I understand you right?*

CARLOS: *Yeah, I feel heard. I know you see it differently, though.*

JANELLE: *Well, yeah! You are my family, sweetheart! The way I see it, money my parents want to give me is really going to us. We should both benefit. You've always been so uncomfortable with it; I was like, "Well okay! I'll buy new shoes!" But you know I don't really feel that way, and I try to show you that by being willing to move money they've given me into our savings account when we need it.*

CARLOS: *It feels good to hear you say that, even if it's hard for me to agree with you....*

After their discussion, here's how Carlos and Janelle redrew their money flow:

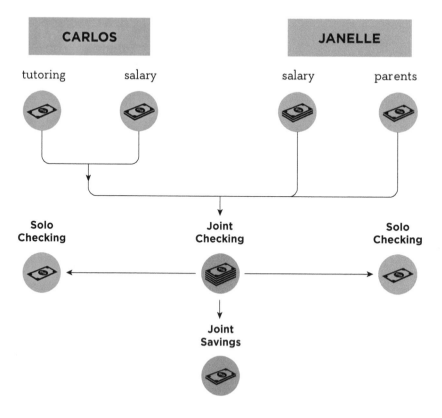

Your turn! How might your money flow work after changing things that aren't working? Redraw your money flow through accounts—where does your income come from and how does it merge and divide? Use the colors red, blue, and purple as described earlier.

Spending and Saving Habits

Whether you're buying groceries, purchasing a new car, paying down debt, or investing in a retirement account, the outcome is the same—it's money out the door. But differences of opinion between you and your partner around what you spend money on and how much you save can cause enormous conflict.

ASSESS YOUR SPENDING AND SAVING HABITS

Assess your current spending and saving habits. Use the circle below to draw a pie chart of your spending and savings categories (for example, living expenses, entertainment, pet care, retirement contributions, wellness/health, and so on). Do you want to make any shifts in the size of your slices?

BUDGET PRIORITIES

Usually, when it comes to budget priorities, opposites attract. These priorities come from the attitudes we hold about money, the lessons we learned about money from our families and our early earning experiences, and our personal beliefs about the best ways to handle money. Did you choose a partner who prioritizes spending in a way that's opposite from the way that you do?

DETERMINE YOUR BUDGET PRIORITIES

Answer True or False to the following statements, and then compare your priorities with your partner's.

Which answers are the same, and which are different? Use the communication skills from step 1 to deepen your understanding of your partner's perspective.

T / F I would rather spend money on experiences (travel, going out to eat) than things (new TV, gifts).

T / F I choose thrifty (on sale, second-hand stores) over expensive (all-organic, name brands).

T / F I value high-risk/high-reward investments over low-risk/low-reward investments.

T / F I prefer to keep my savings liquid (CDs, stock market) versus illiquid (real estate, bonds).

T / F I would rather pay someone for help (housecleaner, mechanic) than do it myself (mow my own lawn, paint my own house).

Does your budget reflect your values?

_____

_____

_____

_____

Does your budget leave enough money to meet your spending and savings habits?

_____

_____

_____

_____

DEBT

The reasons couples carry debt are varied, and debt itself is not inherently a good or bad thing. Debt can be a way to invest in your future, such as taking out a loan to pay for education or a mortgage to buy a house. Debt can be a way to expand your buying power, such as buying a new appliance on credit instead of depleting your cash. But debt can also cause stress, like when accumulated interest overwhelms your ability to pay the principal. Or it can damage your future buying power, such as when your credit score is too low to qualify for a loan or lease.

EXAMINE VIEWS ON PERSONAL DEBT

Have you disclosed your personal debt to your partner?

_____

_____

_____

_____

Do you know your credit score, and have you shared it with your partner?

_____

_____

_____

_____

What are your opinions on carrying debt? Does your answer depend on the kind of debt? For example, do you view carrying a balance on a credit card differently than making the minimum payments on a student loan each month?

_____

_____

_____

_____

Look back over the discussions and exercises in this chapter. What did you learn? What are the important new ideas for you? How will you use them to strengthen your marriage?

_____

_____

_____

_____

How are you feeling? How is your partner feeling? What are the similarities and differences in how you're feeling? (See appendix A for help with identifying your feelings.)

_____

_____

_____

_____

ACTION ITEMS

Here are specific actions you can take to implement the lessons and ideas you learned in this chapter:

1 Make a joint donation to a charity or cause you both care about.
2 Plan a mini-vacation, such as a day trip or overnight stay, and determine the budget together. During the trip, take a picture or purchase a memento to remind you of the time together.
3 Take a financial literacy course or meet with a financial planner.
4 Devote an hour a week to discussing marital finances, such as upcoming bills or revising savings amounts.
5 Buy each other a present—just because!

EXPLORE INTIMACY

Intimacy issues are as common as they are distressing—especially when they get tangled up with other problem areas in the marriage. Problems in areas like communication, respect, and priority filter into problems with sex, and vice versa. The result is a sexless marriage plagued by arguments, resentment, and loneliness. Yikes!

For some couples, intimacy issues are what bring them to therapy. But more often, problems in the bedroom are revealed only when I specifically ask about sex. At first there is uncomfortable shifting on the couch and sideways glances. But once couples get to talking about what's not going well and how they wish it could be different and come to understand there are solutions, there is palpable relief. *Sex matters. We will find each other again.*

Although there is a general discomfort in our culture (and often in our own minds) when talking about sex, it is a central and important component of marriage that must be addressed. I'm going to use the "real" words to talk about sex and body parts. Yes, *lovemaking* is a beautiful phrase, but I don't think softening language is helpful here, especially when euphemisms are often tinted with shame and inhibition. My goal is to help you assess, problem solve, and communicate clearly about sex in your marriage. Although I use the word *sex* throughout the chapter, I'm not just referring to penetrative intercourse. Feel free to substitute for the word *sex* whatever other sexual behaviors make sense in the context of your relationship. You and your partner should finish this chapter with an expanded sexual vocabulary and a sex-positive outlook.

If you've been experiencing physical pain associated with sex, or if any of the exercises in this chapter cause pain in your genitals, please consult with a medical provider. Pain is a signal that your body needs help, and that needs to be taken seriously. Sexual pain is not "all in your head." And there are effective treatments and techniques that can relieve sexual pain.

Take a moment to fill in the areas of strength and conflict from your everyday issues assessment (page 11) that will guide your focus in this step.

Step 3: Explore Intimacy

Strengths _____ and _____

Conflicts _____ and _____

Sex and Marriage

We put quite a bit of pressure on marriage these days—our partners are supposed to be many people in one person: our best friend, our business partner, our co-parent, and our passionate lover. They are supposed to know us intimately and still find us interesting. They are supposed to be able to see us at our worst and still find us attractive. In marriage, we long for security and comfort, and simultaneously for desire and passion. And often, the very intimacy we crave and the familiarity that makes marriage safe are exactly the conditions that stifle eroticism and desire, which require a mysterious mix of intrigue and risk.

There are many facets to what makes sex good for both partners—satisfaction, frequency, fantasy, and desire. Before we dive in to each of those topics more deeply, here's a quick 10-question sexual assessment.

IDENTIFY SEXUAL ISSUES

Answer True or False to each of the following statements, and then compare your answers with your partner's:

T/F It's easy for me to become sexually aroused when I think about someone I find attractive or when I fantasize about sex.

T/F Only under specific conditions do I become interested in having sex, only when everything is "just right."

T/F I believe that my body is desirable and attractive.

T/F Masturbation is enjoyable, and I can bring myself to orgasm.

T/F Anxious thoughts often invade my sexual experience and inhibit arousal.

T/F I feel comfortable asking for what I need and want during sex.

T/F I feel comfortable sharing feedback with my partner after sex.

T/F My partner knows which specific sexual acts make me uncomfortable and why.

T/F Pornography/erotic fantasy features prominently in my sexual experiences.

T/F Sex deepens my sense of bonding and relationship satisfaction.

UNWANTED SEXUAL ENCOUNTERS

If you or your partner has ever experienced unwanted sexual encounters—such as sexual harassment, sexual assault, or sexual abuse—you are not alone. As discussions of intimacy problems unfold, many couples in my practice share stories of sexual trauma. Unwanted sexual attention from colleagues, enduring catcalls while walking down the street, early exposure to sexually explicit images as children, forced sexual encounters, and so on are traumatic experiences. The aftermath is often deeply painful and can last for years after the event occurred, affecting intimacy with your current partner.

Individual or couples therapy can be profoundly healing for sexual trauma. There is nothing wrong with you. You are not broken. You are worthy of love and respect. You are capable of reclaiming the power of your body and of your voice. Help is available to you.

FEELINGS AND REFLECTION

How did you feel answering the preceding questions? Intrigued, embarrassed, proud? How did your partner feel? (See appendix A for help with identifying your feelings.)

_____

_____

_____

_____

Did any of your answers surprise you? Did any of your partner's answers surprise you?

_____

_____

_____

_____

Where are your answers aligned, and where do they differ?

_____

_____

_____

_____

Do the problems in your sex life arise in the areas where you're aligned or where you're different?

_____

_____

_____

_____

FURTHER EXPLORATION

What do you value most about sex in your marriage (intimacy, stress release, conflict resolution, etc.)?

_____

_____

_____

_____

What kinds of touching do you prefer (firm or soft, rubbing or squeezing, simultaneous or taking turns, etc.)?

_____

_____

_____

_____

What aspects of intercourse are most pleasurable (position, type of thrusting, speed, etc.)?

_____

_____

_____

_____

What external stimulations are erotic to you (sensory restriction/blindfolding, sensory enhancement/vibration, sensory diversity/talking dirty, etc.)?

_____

_____

_____

_____

What does it take for you to initiate sex (personal desire, perceived partner receptivity, physical signs of arousal, etc.)?

_____

_____

_____

_____

Sexual Satisfaction

Sexual satisfaction is a broad concept for a complex experience: there are personal factors and partner factors, factors about how the two of you interact and how you communicate, and factors about your setting and context. Let's explore each of these factors more specifically.

THE ROLE OF STRESS

Stress reduces sexual pleasure in almost everyone—the physiological body responses to stress can directly undermine the physiological body response to desire. Managing the stressors in your life and developing stronger antidotes to your stress response will increase sexual satisfaction.

> TIM SAYS: *"Looking back over the years of my marriage, I can tell that stress affected our sex in bad ways. Sometimes Linda would initiate, and even though I'd had an intensely stressful day at a job site, I'd go for it. The result was quick, passionless sex that disappointed both of us. And other times, Linda would initiate and I'd say no. That was how we really knew things were crazy at work. Most of the time, stress meant sex didn't happen at all."*

COPING WITH STRESS

Select a current stressor that is critical for you right now. (By critical, I mean that resolving the stressor is a high priority and that you have the ability to make meaningful changes toward a resolution.)

Stressor: _____

How do you know this stressor is stressing you out? (Consider how your body is responding, how your emotions are affected, and how your partner notices your stress.)

_____

_____

_____

_____

Brainstorm 10 strategies, behavior changes, or solutions that would make a difference. (Don't censor your list. Even solutions that don't seem plausible belong here. Get creative! And don't leave off strategies that your partner could help you implement.)

1 _____

2 _____

3 _____

4 _____

5 _____

6 _____

7 _____

8 _____

9 _____

10 _____

Circle one or two solutions from your list. How committed are you to doing what it will take to implement these strategies, or getting the help you need to implement them?

> *I can come up with — — — — — I'll do whatever it takes.*
> *a million excuses.*

PRACTICE STRESS-REDUCING SOLUTIONS

Over the next few weeks, make intentional and meaningful efforts to put the solutions you chose from your list into practice. Enlist the help of your partner, family, and friends to help you be successful in reducing your stress response or managing the stressor differently.

Notice differences in your mood, physical health, and relationship. Notice differences in your experience of masturbation, of sex with your partner, and of orgasm. What do you notice?

_____

_____

_____

_____

THE ROLE OF FEEDBACK

Giving feedback to your partner after a sexual encounter is another way to improve sexual satisfaction. Your partner may be very in tune with you, but they're still not a mind reader! Use assertive communication to share feedback about what you liked and what you didn't so that satisfaction increases the next time you have sex. Be open to receiving such feedback from your partner, too.

One reason we avoid sharing feedback or asking our partner for something different is because we want to avoid hurting their feelings or criticizing their efforts. It's important to be sensitive, but not avoidant—you are the best teacher for your partner about what turns you on and turns you off, and vice versa. Try reframing your request as an alternative, first clearly stating what you don't want and specifically asking for what you would like instead. For example, "Instead of pinching my nipples with your fingers, I'd like you to suck on them," or "Instead of light touching on my back, I'd like you to use more pressure."

MEI-LIN SAYS: *"Beth often accuses me of being the sensitive one in our relationship, but let me tell you—when it comes to getting feedback about sex with me, SHE is SUPER sensitive. When I've tried to tell her what I like and don't like, she gets defensive and takes it personally. And then I have to do damage control! It's just not worth telling her. I'd rather just endure something I don't like than cause a fight. It's not that bad . . ."*

REFRAME REQUESTS FOR CHANGE

Take turns with your partner exchanging requests using the following prompt. Remember to use your communication skills from step 1.

Instead of _____, I'd like _____.

Instead of _____, I'd like _____.

Instead of _____, I'd like _____.

Instead of _____, I'd like _____.

PRACTICE GIVING FEEDBACK

Try to make feedback a regular part of sex. Instead of giving feedback only when you have something "negative" to say or when you're asking for a different sexual technique or experience, making feedback a regular part of sex reduces the association of feedback with complaints.

After your next sexual encounter, practice sharing with each other about your experience—the good and the awkward and the not so good. Express gratitude, laugh, and let the information you learn from your partner influence how sex goes the next time. How did it go?

_____

_____

_____

_____

THE ROLE OF CONTEXT

I can't stress enough the power of context in regard to sexual satisfaction. Small shifts one way or another way, softer or harder, faster or slower, can be the difference between ecstasy and irritation. It's true! The same behavior or sensation in different contexts can have a dramatically different effect. Here are some examples to demonstrate the power of context to heighten or dampen satisfaction:

Your partner comes up behind you and smacks your butt.

Location: In your kitchen versus at your parents' house.

You step into the shower and your partner follows you.

Time: 15 minutes before you're running late for work versus when the kids are watching cartoons.

You hear your partner say, "Wow, you look amazing."

Body image: Feeling confident and healthy versus feeling critical and dissatisfied.

BETH SAYS: *"I sympathize with Mei-Lin, I really do—I'm full of contradictions. I'm a needy lover and a confident one. I'm hot then cold, passionately giving and then self-focused. One minute her kisses are sensual; the next minute I'm irritated by the traffic noise outside. One minute the wine helps me relax and feel sexy; the next minute I'm too tipsy to orgasm. I wish I could figure out how to get more consistency for myself, and for sex with my sweetheart."*

As you're starting to see, context involves personal factors, relationship factors, situational factors, and behavioral factors. The next exercise is a big one—it's probably going to take a while to complete. But it's worth the effort. Learning about the contexts that contribute to your high-satisfaction and low-satisfaction sexual experiences is an important step in being able to intentionally create contexts for sex that satisfy you and your partner. Fill out the Explore High-Satisfaction and Low-Satisfaction Contexts exercise on the next few pages, then come back and answer these questions.

EXPLORE HIGH-SATISFACTION AND LOW-SATISFACTION CONTEXTS

Think back to two occasions when you and your partner had sex—one in which you felt immensely satisfied and one in which you felt unsatisfied—and try to remember all the factors involved. Then fill out this worksheet as best as you can.

Describe a **positive, high-satisfaction** sexual experience with your partner:

_____

_____

_____

_____

Explore the factors that contributed to that positive experience:

_____

_____

_____

_____

Personal factors (physical health, mental health, body image, energy level, etc.):

_____

_____

_____

_____

Partner factors (physical health, mental health, body image, energy level, etc.):

_____

_____

_____

_____

Setting factors (location, temperature, noise, scents, time, events preceding and following, etc.):

_____

_____

_____

_____

Relationship dynamic factors (risk/trust, power/control, leading/following, stress/relaxation, etc.):

_____

_____

_____

_____

Behavior factors (body parts, fantasy, stimulation, toys, position, etc.):

_____

_____

_____

_____

Describe a **negative, low-satisfaction** sexual experience with your partner:

_____

_____

_____

_____

Explore the factors that contributed to that negative experience:

_____

_____

_____

_____

Personal factors (physical health, mental health, body image, energy level, etc.):

_____

_____

_____

_____

Partner factors (physical health, mental health, body image, energy level, etc.):

_____

_____

_____

_____

Setting factors (location, temperature, noise, scents, time, events preceding and following, etc.):

_____

_____

_____

_____

Relationship dynamic factors (risk/trust, power/control, leading/following, stress/relaxation, etc.):

_____

_____

_____

_____

Behavior factors (body parts, fantasy, stimulation, toys, position, etc.):

_____

_____

_____

_____

Are you surprised by any of your answers in the previous exercise?

_____

_____

_____

Are you surprised by your partner's answers?

_____

_____

_____

Where are your answers aligned, and where do they differ?

_____

_____

_____

Do the problems in your sex life arise in the areas where you're aligned or where you're different?

_____

_____

_____

THE ROLE OF FREQUENCY

The most common complaints I hear about frequency of sex are that it doesn't happen frequently enough or that one partner wants more frequent sex than the other. The longer in between sexual encounters, the more difficult it feels to initiate anew. If sex is a train, it's a heavy one—and once it slows down, or comes to a complete stop, the momentum required to get the wheels turning again can feel effortful. And that effort can lead to awkwardness, fear of rejection, and a likelihood of saying, "Not tonight."

LINDA SAYS: *"When I think about the word frequency in regards to sex with Tim, I just laugh. Is 'never' a frequency? The longer we go without having sex, the less likely it seems we'll ever have it. And don't get me wrong. I want to! And I know Tim wants to! But we just don't. And then we just keep not having sex, and then before we know what's happened it's been months."*

The following two exercises explore these two aspects of frequency: How much is enough sex, and how do you transition from not having sex to having sex?

TAKE THE "GOLDILOCKS TEST"

How different are your views about the ideal frequency of sex? Fill out the worksheet below to find out.

"This porridge is too cold."	"This porridge is too hot."	"This porridge is just right."
What frequency of sex leaves you longing for more?	*What frequency of sex leaves you wanting a break?*	*What frequency of sex leaves you satisfied?*

Are you surprised by any of your answers? Are you surprised by your partner's answers? Where are your answers aligned, and where do they differ?

_____

_____

_____

_____

Do the problems in your sex life arise in the areas where you're aligned or where you're different?

_____

_____

_____

_____

EXPLORE INITIATION STRATEGIES

How do you initiate sex?

_____

_____

_____

_____

How do you know your partner wants to have sex?

_____

_____

_____

_____

How do you respond when your partner says no?

_____

_____

_____

_____

How do you say no? How do you say yes?

_____

_____

_____

_____

What about the initiation experience do you want to be different?

_____

_____

_____

_____

THE ROLE OF PORNOGRAPHY AND FANTASY

The role of pornography and erotic fantasy is essential to talk about within a marriage. In my counseling with couples, I focus on two aspects: the underlying desires and turn-ons within the images or fantasies, and whether the pornography or fantasy propels the partners toward each other or away from each other.

JANELLE SAYS: *"The other day, Carlos left his computer unlocked, and I glanced at the windows open in his browser. Immediately, I knew what I was looking at: images of naked women on beaches, touching themselves. I'm not upset that he masturbates (I do that, too) or that he looks at images while he does (I 'look' at images in my head through my fantasy). But I find myself filled with self-doubt now. I'm afraid that because I don't look like those women, I'm not enough for him, that I have to be like those images to be sexy to him."*

Call to mind recent images or videos you've viewed, or the fantasy you've imagined in your mind's eye. Beyond the body parts, sounds, and sexual acts that you see, what else is erotic and desirable to you? (For example: Is it that the person in the fantasy never says no? Is it that the person in the fantasy is confident and assertive? Is it that you have full control of what happens in your own body during the erotic fantasy experience?)

_____

_____

_____

_____

Now, take what you've discovered as desirable within the fantasy and relate it to sex with your partner. What would it take to incorporate this aspect into your erotic experiences with each other? What are the ways that the pornography or fantasy, and how it makes you feel, can increase the satisfaction of sex in real life?

_____

_____

_____

_____

SHARE A FANTASY

Describe a fantasy, romantic or sexual, that you'd like to experience with your partner. Include things like where you are and how it feels as it gets going. Describe what happens first, then next, then after that. Include descriptions of where you touch each other and what you say to each other. Write a satisfactory ending. Also describe what this fantasy means to you and how you would feel if it came true.

_____

_____

_____

_____

Scheduling Sex

Many couples find it difficult to make time for the relaxed, passionate, lingering sex they enjoyed while dating. Work is busy, kids require energy, and there are dishes to wash and laundry to put away, and the list goes on . . . and by the time you fall into bed at night, you're asleep before your head hits the pillow.

Scheduling sex is a way to carve out the time on your calendars to prioritize sex in your marriage amid all the other activities and tasks on your lists. But most people balk at the idea of scheduling sex. I'm guessing that you want it to be spontaneous. Really, though, was sex ever spontaneous? I think what you mean is that it felt natural, it flowed easily, and it was wanted by both people at the same time. Of course you knew you were going to have sex when you got together after work! You were thinking about it all day, you shaved your legs or your face that morning on purpose, and you wore something special that made you feel desirable. So when you finally made it into each other's arms, sex wasn't spontaneous, was it? It was actually pretty much planned. You expected it to happen and you couldn't wait.

JOSH SAYS: *"Heather and I have trouble making time for sex. We get up at different times in the morning, and by the end of a long day at work (for me) or a long day with the kids (for her), we're often too tired to have sex before bed. We've tried scheduling sex on our calendars, and that sort of worked in that we 'got it done,' but it didn't feel the same to me. I want sex to be special again, like it was before kids or like when we were in college. I want it to be spontaneous and sexy!"*

HEATHER SAYS: *"I often feel so much pressure to have sex with Josh, like it's another thing on my long list of things to do. And by the end of the day, it's not so much that I'm tired (I definitely am, but I could get over that for good sex), it's that I'm overtouched. All day long I have the baby in my arms and on my breast, and I have an active kid jumping and climbing around me like a jungle gym. I want sex with Josh, but more often my longing for keeping my body to myself wins out."*

MAKE SEX A RITUAL

It's not the scheduling itself that's the problem, it's the meaning behind the scheduling. If you think of it as scheduling a routine, like every Tuesday morning you take the trash out to the curb, sex will feel like an obligation, a task to cross off the to-do list. A routine can be effective, but it's not special. So shift from thinking about scheduling sex like *routine* to thinking about scheduling sex like *ritual*. A ritual is something you look forward to: "Ooh, won't it be so nice to have time to ourselves Monday evening while the kids are at piano lessons?"

The time a ritual takes up in your day is something that you protect: "Thanks for the invite to brunch, but we already have plans Saturday morning!" A ritual is fantasized about before it happens ("I can't wait!"), and the anticipation sparks desire and arousal and heightens the experience when it's finally time to enjoy your time together. And it's reminisced about after it's over ("Wasn't that worth it?"), so the enjoyment and pleasure linger into the routines of life that come afterward.

SCHEDULE SEX AS A WEEKLY RITUAL

Look at your calendars and find one or two times during the week to schedule sex. Is there a reliable time you're alone together? What do you need to do earlier in the day or the week to protect that time and to be ready for sex when the time comes?

_____

_____

_____

_____

Nonsexual Touching (Affection)

Intimacy in a marriage isn't just all about sex. Physical touch is an important part of feeling close, deepening intimacy, and expressing love. But when it's difficult to connect sexually, because of infrequent sex or unsatisfying sex, often all types of physical touch fall away. It's important to remember that touch has meaning beyond foreplay, and that nonsexual touching is a way of showing affection in your marriage. And intimacy and affection aren't always touching—it's also feeling loved, close, and accepted as a whole person.

CARLOS SAYS: *"Janelle and I fight about sex all the time. Well, actually, we fight about what happens before sex. She's always accusing me of pushing sex on her, and that makes me crazy—I like touching my wife! I want to kiss her and hold her and put my hand down her shirt! So sue me. But I don't always want sex; sometimes I just want to play, to touch. We go around and around and get angrier and angrier. I feel misunderstood. She feels used. It's bad, bad, bad. I miss just touching her body, enjoying her skin and her hair."*

RECEIVING AND SHOWING AFFECTION

What are ways you feel loved and accepted by your partner?

_____

_____

_____

What makes you feel that your worth is acknowledged, even as a whole person with failings and imperfections?

_____

_____

_____

Are there different ways you show your partner you love and accept them, acknowledging their worth as a whole person?

_____

_____

_____

WHAT DOES TOUCHING MEAN?

Answer True or False to the following statements, and then compare your answers:

> T / F Sometimes I avoid affection with my partner because I don't want it to lead to sex.
>
> T / F Any kiss more intense than a quick peck goodbye means my partner wants sex.
>
> T / F We're not affectionate just for the sake of pleasure; we're affectionate when we're ready to have sex.
>
> T / F If I don't want to have sex, I don't reach for my partner in bed before sleep.
>
> T / F I miss feeling close while touching without the pressure of doing more.

If you answered True to three or more of the statements, touching has become tangled up with sex to the point that you're suspicious of most affection. Work together to untangle this connection. Use words to explain to each other what your intentions are ("I want to feel close to you and cuddle on the couch") and what your perceptions are ("When you kiss me like that I wonder what you want to do next").

If you answered False to three or more of the statements, touching for the pure sake of touching is a separate experience from touching that leads to sex. There is a spectrum that you both intuit or communicate to each other, from affection to sensuality to sex. Touching energizes your bond, and whether or not it leads to sex, you are able to enjoy physical connection and contact.

Which affectionate behaviors are most pleasurable to you?

_____

_____

_____

_____

How was affection displayed in your family growing up?

_____

_____

_____

_____

How did the affection you received, or didn't receive, influence your past romantic relationships?

_____

_____

_____

_____

How does the affection you experienced growing up influence your experience of affection in your marriage?

_____

_____

_____

_____

WHAT CHARGES YOUR "LOVE BATTERY"

Each of us has a metaphorical "love battery" that is charged by affection and connection from others as well as from ourselves. When it's low, we are likely to be grumpy, clingy, or distant. When it's buzzing with energy, we are more likely to be relaxed, pleasant, and emotionally regulated. This metaphor also helps overcome the vulnerability it takes to ask directly for what you need. Instead of "Can you give me a hug?" you can playfully say, "My love battery is low!"

What are the affectionate, self-care behaviors that charge your love battery? (Some ideas include: positive affirmations like "I am worthy of love," a walk in nature, a hot shower or bath, and laughing.)

_____

_____

_____

What are the affectionate, caring behaviors your partner can do that charge your love battery? (Some ideas include: a hug, cuddling on the couch, holding hands in the car, and love notes.)

_____

_____

_____

PRACTICE CHARGING YOUR LOVE BATTERIES

Discuss the behaviors that charge each of your love batteries to the fullest. This week, practice asking for help with charging your love battery, and practice offering help to your partner. How did it feel to charge your love batteries?

_____

_____

_____

ASK FOR WHAT YOU NEED

One of the classic sex therapy interventions is a technique called *sensate-focused*, or *non-demand*, touch. It means you touch intentionally, but for the sake of pleasure and connection only, not to lead to sex. Here's the premise: The couple schedules a "session" at home, setting aside about an hour or so for the exercise.

- Because erotic touching, orgasm, and intercourse are prohibited, the couple is focused on feelings, sensations, and communication. Non-demand touching is an opportunity to enjoy physical contact without frustration, disappointment, or rejection. Erections, lubrication, and secretions are considered a natural response to pleasure, and are not considered a demand for sexual activity.
- One partner is the giver of touch; the other is the receiver. Both partners are naked. The giver explores their partner's body, savoring physical contact without trying to turn them on. The receiver is passive, receives pleasure, and communicates to the giver which body parts and what types of touching are most pleasurable.
- The couple can explore with sensory-enhancing elements: music, lighting, temperature, fabric, and scents. The giver can explore with touch through different body parts: mouth, tongue, and hands. The giver can explore with different kinds of touch: rubbing, caressing, playing, flicking, sucking, and licking. The receiver can respond with words, sounds, and breathing, but is not to touch the giver back.
- Lying down or lounging on a bed, the giver explores the receiver's body from head to toe, back to front. Focus on each body part like any other, especially exploring genitals as you would an elbow or nipple or finger. If at any point the giver or receiver feels uncomfortable, do not stop touching or avoid contact. Instead, lie still in an embrace until both partners feel relaxed and safe again. Then the non-demand touching continues.
- When the whole body has been explored and the session is drawing to an end, lie together and hold each other. Share feelings, perceptions, responses, requests, and feedback. What did you learn about your body? What did you learn about your partner's body? How can you translate what you've both learned from non-demand touching into sex and intercourse?
- Switch roles, either in the same session or for the next session.

Look back over the discussions and exercises in this chapter. What did you learn? What are the important new ideas for you? How will you use them to strengthen your marriage?

_____

_____

_____

How are you feeling? How is your partner feeling? What are the similarities and differences in how you're feeling? (See appendix A for help with identifying your feelings.)

_____

_____

_____

ACTION ITEMS

Here are specific actions you can take to implement the lessons and ideas you learned in this chapter:

1   Book a couples massage or take turns giving each other full-body massages at home. Enjoy touching for pleasure, but without the expectation of sex.

2   Attend an exercise class or go for a jog together. Get sweaty! Then take a shower or bath together, and take turns washing each other's bodies.

3   Pick out a new perfume or cologne for each other. Use the scent to send signals to each other—strategically wear it when you're interested in having sex, interested in arousing your partner, or when you're feeling intimately attached.

4   Have sex in a place where you've never done it before. Perhaps this is a room in your house or a room in a local hotel. (Make sure both partners are comfortable with the new location!)

5   Create a music playlist together with songs that lead you through a sexual encounter: Start with music that puts you in the mood for sex, then include songs to accompany and heighten sex, and end with songs to keep you connected in the afterglow. Instrumental? Lyrics? Romantic ballads? Hard rock?

REUNITE AS *WE*

It's common for marriage to enter difficult seasons. Of course you love each other and enjoy each other's company, talking about and experiencing the world as a couple. But too often, the busyness of life gets in the way of connection. For some marriages, the problem is too much separateness, too much distance to feel close. If this is you, the phrase "two ships passing in the night" is one you've probably said about your relationship at some point. For other marriages, the problem is too much togetherness, not enough space to feel free. Maybe you're aching for some breathing room to let heated emotions cool.

I designed this step to help you reestablish your marriage to the highest level of priority, reuniting yourselves as a couple without sacrificing your individuality. The core of a marriage is partnership—the balance of separateness and togetherness that feels right to you in your marriage is unique.

Take a moment to fill in the areas of strength and conflict from your everyday issues assessment (page 11) that will guide your focus in this step.

Step 4: Reunite as *We*

Strengths _____ and _____

Conflicts _____ and _____

Live Your Lives Together . . . and Apart

One of the most important ways to establish a strong sense of *we* is to achieve a balance between time together as a couple and time apart. This might seem counterintuitive—*time apart is supposed to help us feel closer?* Exactly!

Although balancing time together and time apart in a relationship can be challenging, it's a really important skill for marriage. For many married couples, separateness and togetherness can feel like oil and water. The good news is independence and connection don't have to be in conflict. I know this may sound like wild relationship advice, but here it is: *Leave and come back.* Here is what I mean:

Go into the world as a unique, whole person. Be aware of your surroundings; be vulnerable and open to new experiences. Be your own person! Follow your own passions! Live your own dreams! Try not to think about your partner when you're gone or feel guilty for the time spent away. These passions, dreams, and the sense of self you obtain when you embrace your own life will infuse energy into your marriage.

And then come back! Come back to each other as unique, whole people. Be aware of what you have learned and share those insights with your partner; be vulnerable with each other and open to a new depth of intimacy. Share your heart! Bare your soul! Remain curious about each other to deepen intimacy and connection. Bring the insights and questions and "aha!" moments back to your partner.

Your time apart restores and affirms your individuality, and your time together when you come back restores and affirms your partnership. It's important to be careful, of course—careful with distance, with time, with company, with intention, and with meaning. Only the two of you know how far away from each other is too far. It takes trust and sensitivity to have a wonderful experience without your partner, and to have that be not just okay, but encouraged and celebrated.

Ultimately, your marriage will be stronger for your individual passions and dreams, for the people you are when you're apart. Because when you bring that energy back to the marriage, using it to deepen your connection and intimacy, it in turn gives you courage and freedom to explore on your own once again.

Mei-Lin wanted to learn how to knit so that she could make a blanket for her sister's new baby. Even though it took hours of watching YouTube videos, she figured it out! One Saturday when Mei-Lin was absorbed in knitting, Beth took care of all the errands. And when she needed to buy more yarn, Mei-Lin bravely introduced herself to the knitting expert at her local crafts store. They ended up going out for coffee and have become friends! Beth feels proud of Mei-Lin for not only learning a new skill but stretching herself socially.

What is something you've always wanted to learn how to do but have not pursued?

_____

_____

_____

_____

What traits or skills will you need to reach for to be successful?

_____

_____

_____

_____

In what ways can your partner support you so that you're able to pursue this passion?

_____

_____

_____

_____

What energy from your pursuit of this passion will you bring back to your relationship? How will your partner benefit from your time away?

_____

_____

_____

_____

DO YOUR OWN THING

The next time you're on a trip or vacation together, consider spending some time on your own doing your own thing (for example, visit a place you're interested in visiting, eat something you've been aching to try, or wander until you find something you weren't sure you were looking for). These separate experiences within your shared experience as a couple can enrich the vacation, bringing new eyes and ears and a smattering of _"Oh, really? Tell me more about that. Wow!"_ to your conversations.

If you don't have a vacation planned, consider spending a few hours apart doing something each of you would enjoy, and then discuss your experiences.

How did it feel to each do your own thing and then come back together and share?

_____

_____

_____

_____

Pay Attention to Each Other

When is the last time you _really looked_ at your partner? Not to judge, criticize, or complain, but to understand, admire, and compliment? Paying attention to each other means that you show caring to your partner when out with friends, that you notice the loving things that they do, and that you keep your partnership central despite the interference of stress.

JANELLE SAYS: *"I think back to when I first saw Carlos's picture come up on the dating app—the first thing I noticed was his eyes. And then, on our first date, when we made eye contact for the first time . . . it was like an electric shock. He didn't even know me, but he was looking at me with such kindness and openness. It's actually like our secret signal. When we're out with friends and feeling disconnected, all we have to do is make eye contact and it's like, 'Oh yeah, there you are.' We should look at each other like that more often."*

PRACTICE THE GAZE

Eyes are the windows to our souls, and gazing into each other's eyes is a way to deepen intimacy and pay attention to each other.

Sit comfortably facing your partner and set a timer for two minutes. The goal is to keep eye contact the entire time, without talking.

For most couples, this experience is intense and often opens up deep feelings of love and connection. Don't be surprised if you feel compelled to reach for one another or cry. See your partner, and open yourself to be seen. How did it go?

_____

_____

_____

_____

Social Styles

Sometimes, like Mei-Lin and Beth, one partner is more introverted and one partner is more extroverted, and other times a couple's social styles will be very similar. Do you and your partner agree on most social outings, or is one of you more likely to talk the other into going to the party—or staying home? The next exercise can help you figure out what you and your partner are most comfortable with when it comes to socializing.

WHAT IS YOUR SOCIAL STYLE?

Take this short quiz to find out whether you're more of an introvert or an extrovert.

1 What is your idea of a great party?
   a) A low-key gathering of close friends, focused on intimate conversation
   b) A high-energy gathering of friends, acquaintances, and new people to meet
2 How do you recharge after a tough day?
   a) Time alone with a book, music, or my own thoughts
   b) Time with my partner or friends in conversation, or doing something together
3 Which are you more afraid of?
   a) Being outside my comfort zone or around people who don't know me
   b) Feeling isolated from my friends or not having someone to talk to
4 Where is your partner at a party in relation to you?
   a) Right by my side, holding my hand
   b) Doing their own thing, having fun!
5 When out in public together, is it okay to show affection to your partner?
   a) I prefer to keep affection private and intimate, rather than public and showy.
   b) Showing affection around other people is fun and a way to demonstrate I care; I don't mind the attention we might get from others.

If you answered mostly *a*, your social style tends more toward introversion, and you get your energy from introspective time with yourself or close friends. You enjoy one-on-one conversations and feel comfortable sharing when someone is actively listening.

If you answered mostly *b*, your social style tends more toward extroversion, and you get your energy from exuberant time with close friends, as well as with new people who could become friends. You enjoy conversations with (almost) anyone and feel comfortable asserting yourself into a group.

Compare your quiz answers with your partner's answers. Remember, being different (complementary!) doesn't always cause problems, just like being the same doesn't always go smoothly.

How are your social styles similar or different?

_____

_____

_____

_____

How do these similarities or differences strengthen your partnership?

_____

_____

_____

_____

How do they cause problems?

_____

_____

_____

_____

EXPRESS GRATITUDE

One really positive way to pay attention to your partner is to express gratitude. Being able to express gratitude means that you're focusing on the good qualities in your partner—helpfulness, generosity, teamwork—and that you're willing to share appreciation.

Split a pack of sticky notes in half—half a pack for each of you. Leave short messages to each other on the sticky notes, thanking each other for something. The first step is to actually notice the good, helpful, loving things your partner is doing. And the next step is to express gratitude for these things.

Leave the notes in fun places, like tucked into a briefcase or stuck to the bathroom mirror. Collect the notes your partner leaves for you. How does it feel to look for positive behaviors? How does it feel to be thanked for your efforts at a loving partnership?

_____

_____

_____

_____

The Role of Stress in Connection

If you're like most people, it's likely that you're pretty stressed out most of the time. And feeling stress often inhibits connection. It blinds us to our partner's experience, prevents us from expressing empathy, and overfocuses us on our own problems. Although avoiding the situations that create stress may not be possible, we are able to control our responses to those situations. One way to think about this is that different people experience different triggers of stress. (Heather gets stressed when she—or anybody!—is running late, but running late doesn't bother Josh at all.) Becoming more mindful of our reactions to what is happening helps us avoid feeling overwhelmed by stress.

Both negative events (like having a fight with a friend or being unprepared for a fast-approaching deadline) and positive events (like having a baby or planning a vacation) can lead to feeling stress. It's not the event itself but rather your emotional response to that event that causes stress.

THE DIFFERENCE BETWEEN STRESS AND ANXIETY/DEPRESSION

Stress is your body's response to a change in your environment or context. When you feel stressed, that's your body reacting to positive or negative change—falling in love, starting a new project, or suffering an unexpected disappointment—with physical, mental, and emotional responses. Anxiety is a mental state that's characterized by feelings of apprehension, nervousness, or fear. When anxiety takes over and interferes with your life or relationships, you might feel overwhelmed by uneasiness and experience distressing behaviors like panic attacks. Depression is a mental state that's characterized by feelings of sadness, hopelessness, or malaise. Depression manifests itself as low energy or motivation, difficulty sleeping or sleeping too much, and changes in appetite.

An experienced mental health professional can help you determine whether you are experiencing stress, which is a normal (if sometimes uncomfortable) response to change, or anxiety or depression symptoms, which can become too frequent or forceful to cope with on your own.

Mei-Lin says, "I've been seeing an individual counselor for a while now. I know I'm prone to ruminate about things, so sorting out my feelings with her is helpful. I have the skills now to identify the ways my body responds to stress at work (I lose my appetite) or stress with Beth (my heart rate races and I feel like I can't catch my breath), and the difference between when my response is normal and when it's fueled by my anxiety. Sessions are a safe place to process my reactions so that I can talk to my boss or to Beth with more confidence and vulnerability."

IDENTIFY YOUR CURRENT STRESSORS

In this worksheet, make a list of the events in your life, both positive and negative, that are stressful for you right now, and then compare your lists. Are you surprised by anything on your partner's list, and vice versa? Discuss why you perceive these stressors as positive or negative.

Positive Stressors	Negative Stressors
_____	_____
_____	_____
_____	_____
_____	_____

IDENTIFY YOUR SYMPTOMS OF STRESS

Check the symptoms of stress you may notice in your body and your mind, or write in your own. Compare your list to your partner's. Do you experience stress the same or differently?

- ☐ Avoiding friends or recreational activities
- ☐ Being tired and having trouble sleeping
- ☐ Experiencing changes in sleeping and eating habits
- ☐ Feeling agitated or irritable
- ☐ Feeling nervous or anxious
- ☐ Feeling overwhelmed
- ☐ Feeling sad or down
- ☐ Having negative thoughts
- ☐ Having trouble concentrating
- ☐ Increased conflict with family members or friends
- ☐ Increased heart rate
- ☐ Pit in your stomach or a "bad" gut feeling
- ☐ Procrastinating or neglecting responsibilities
- ☐ Quick, shallow breathing
- ☐ Sweaty palms
- ☐ Upset stomach or indigestion

_____

_____

_____

_____

The Role of Technology in Connection

Technology is one of the most common ways we avoid connection with our partner—both intentionally and unintentionally. So it's important to establish rules for use of your phones, tablets, and other devices when with your partner. Mismatches in expectations about technology can cause serious conflict, as this exchange between Heather and Josh illustrates:

HEATHER: *Josh, can you help me with Lucy for a minute? She needs a bath.*

JOSH: *Mhmm (looking down at his phone).*

HEATHER: *(looks over at Josh, sees him looking at his phone) Josh? Please?*

JOSH: *Yeah, coming (still looking at his phone).*

HEATHER: *Josh! Seriously, what is happening on Facebook right now that is so important?*

JOSH: *Why do you always assume I'm looking at social media? I was reading work emails. Give me a break.*

HEATHER: *I don't care what you're doing. I just want you to participate. You're always on your damn phone.*

JOSH: *Don't swear in front of the kids, Heather! And like you aren't? How many times have you checked Instagram today? I have to work. Things at the office are crazy.*

HEATHER: *Yeah, right, things are always crazy. I'm not having this argument with you right now. I'm taking Lucy upstairs for a bath.*

JOSH: *Stop it. I'm here now. What do you want me to do?*

HEATHER: *Nothing. You're obviously too busy.*

(Pop quiz: How many destructive patterns of communication can you identify in that exchange? See page 61 if you need a refresher.)

Together, decide the answers to these questions. (I use the word *phones* below to simplify the question, but insert any other type of technology that is appropriate for your situation.)

- Should we take our phones into the bedroom at night?
- When is it okay to look at our phones during a meal?
- Even if our phones are secure, should each of us have the password to the other's phone?
- What are the top three apps each of us uses on our phones?
- Do we have any concerns about the role of technology in our marriage?

Nurture Your Relationship

To nurture is to cherish, cultivate, and support. To nurture a marriage is to make intentional efforts to repair the damage after a fight, to intentionally demonstrate love through actions, and to invest in fun times together. But like the flight attendant on an airplane tells us, we have to put on our own oxygen masks before helping someone else put on theirs. You will be able to nurture your marriage only to the extent that you are living your life as the best version of yourself as a partner.

CREATE A NURTURING STATEMENT

Fill in the blanks in the sentences below and then share your answers with each other using the skills of effective communication from step 1 (page 60).

"If I were living my life as the best version of myself as a partner that I could be, I would continue to _____; I would do _____ differently. You would know that I am nurturing our marriage because _____, and I hope you would feel more _____."

MARRIAGE VALUES IN ACTION

Think back to your assessment of the values that guide your marriage (from chapter 1, page 8). Write down the qualities you ranked as your top three, then brainstorm behaviors that nurture your relationship and demonstrate those values in action. Here are two examples, from Linda and Tim, to help you get started:

LINDA

VALUE, RANK 1: *Friendship*

BEHAVIORS: *I'm paying more attention to how Tim answers questions about his day, making sure that I listen with my heart; the other day I offered to go to the driving range with him and hit golf balls, since I know how much he loves to play golf. I'm communicating better, and we're having fun together.*

TIM

VALUE, RANK 1: *Passion*

BEHAVIORS: *I learned so much in step 3 about Linda's desire and what she wants sex to be like. Even though we've been having sex for 30-plus years, we were just going through the motions. But now, I'm paying attention to her sexual satisfaction in ways I haven't done since we were newlyweds. And I'm asking for feedback directly, lovingly. Talking about sex is uncomfortable to me, but man—it sure sparks passion for Linda!*

Value, Rank 1: _____

Behaviors: _____

_____

_____

_____

_____

Value, Rank 2: _____

Behaviors: _____

_____

_____

_____

Value, Rank 3: _____

Behaviors: _____

_____

_____

_____

HAVING FUN TOGETHER

Having fun together as a couple is one of the easiest ways to nurture your marriage. Whether you're home watching a movie, at a concert enjoying live music, or traveling abroad, quality time together infuses your relationship with adventure, entertainment, and laughter.

AFTER AN "OOPS CONVERSATION": 5 WAYS TO REPAIR CONNECTION

One of the ways you and your partner nurture your relationship is to prioritize restoring connection after a conversation or interaction derails. Here are five ways to repair connection:

1 Acknowledge your role in the conversation going haywire. For example, "I provoked you when I said you were acting just like your mother. I know that really gets under your skin, and I said it anyway because I was feeling mad. Things took a turn for the worse after I said that."

2 Apologize sincerely for the hurt you caused. For example, "I said some things last night that hurt your feelings. I'm sorry I let my frustration get out of hand. Even if we disagree about something, I don't want to hurt your feelings. I'm really sorry."

3 Plan a date to reconnect. For example, "Let's get a babysitter and go out to dinner tonight. I think getting out of the house and away from the kids for a while will help us reconnect. I know when we feel more relaxed with each other, our conversations tend to go better. Maybe we can try to talk about it again at the restaurant?"

4 Show love through acts of kindness. For example, write a love note, offer affection, help in a meaningful way around the house, or run an errand.

5 Reconnect through affection and sexual intimacy (when both partners are ready). For example, give each other a massage, take a shower together, make out, or have sex.

REMEMBER PAST FUN

What have been your favorite events or vacations together?

_____

_____

_____

_____

Would any of the details of these experiences be easy to replicate now?

_____

_____

_____

_____

Which details seem too difficult to replicate? What can you replace those specific details with to create another memorable experience?

_____

_____

_____

_____

DATE-NIGHT BRAINSTORM

Think about your relationship as it is now—and what you're working hard to help it become. What do you enjoy doing together as a couple that you want to do more of? What do you enjoy doing together as a family if you have children? Use the prompts below to brainstorm a list of potential outings or dates.

1 **Research a list of best local eateries** (for example, restaurants, food trucks, or breweries). Of the ones you've never tried, each of you pick one and then agree on another together. List the three choices below, and commit to trying a new one each month for the next three months:

Partner 1 choice: _____

Partner 2 choice: _____

Joint choice: _____

2 **Research a list of best local attractions** (for example, parks, museums, concert venues). Of the ones you've never been to, each of you pick one and then agree on another together. List the three choices below, and commit to planning to go to a new one each month for the next three months:

Partner 1 choice: _____

Partner 2 choice: _____

Joint choice: _____

SHAKE UP YOUR NEXT DINNER DATE NIGHT

Don't get stuck in a date-night rut! Here are three ideas for how to shake up your next dinner date night:

1   **Meet at the restaurant.** Skip the mundane experience of getting ready together in the same room: "Can you pass me my deodorant?" "Where is my blue shirt?" Instead, get ready separately or meet after work. Rekindle the excitement and anticipation of walking into a crowded restaurant, searching the room for each other, and locking eyes. *It's you!* Let the sparks fly!

2   **Make an early dinner reservation.** Let the babysitter handle the kids' dinner and bedtime, and come home late enough that they're asleep but early enough to have energy for round two of your date at home! What would you like to do next? Eat dessert? Watch a movie? Make out on the couch? How about all of the above? Instead of getting home too tired for anything but falling into bed, you'll be able to build on the positive momentum of a delicious dinner and stimulating conversation when you get home.

3   **Stay in "couple mode" when you get home.** Only one of you needs to check in with the babysitter, to pay them and ask about how the kids behaved and what time they went to sleep. The other one should head straight for the bedroom! Tidy up, light a candle, and change into something that makes you feel attractive. The goal is to keep the energy flirty and romantic, building on the connection you generated at dinner. Once the sitter is on their way home, join each other in the bedroom.

COUPLE FRIENDS AND MENTOR COUPLES

Sometimes marriage feels hard because of the "echo chamber" effect—it's just the two of you going around and around about the same problems. Developing relationships with other couples, both as friendships and mentorships, is one way to break out of destructive patterns. Paying attention to healthy behaviors of other couples can help nurture your relationship.

Couple friends are pairs of partners you have fun with, who are in a similar developmental relationship stage as you. Mentor couples provide a living example of the kind of marriage you want for yourself; they are often a developmental relationship stage beyond you, and you seek them out for advice and guidance.

YOUR COUPLE FRIENDS QUIZ

To determine if your couple friends are healthy for your relationship, answer True or False to the following statements:

> T / F Our friends respect each of us as individuals.
>
> T / F Our friends encourage us to stay married and work through our problems.
>
> T / F Our friends share our interests and values.
>
> T / F When we're with our friends, my partner and I are kind to each other.
>
> T / F When we're with our friends, I like how my partner behaves, and vice versa.

If you answered False to any of these questions, think about why you choose to be with these particular people and how you can improve the relationship so that you can answer True the next time around.

CARLOS SAYS: *"Janelle's parents. Wow, I can't believe I just wrote them down! But even though I resist their influence in many ways, if I'm really honest with myself, Janelle's parents really are a good example of marriage. Compared to my parents, who fight passionately and loudly, her parents are calm and respectful to each other. Her dad really makes an effort to be home for dinner, like my dad didn't do. And even though her mom is (too) involved in our life, I know she really believes in us."*

Who are your role models for healthy relationships? List the names of mentor couples below, and think about the following questions: How do they speak to each other, particularly when they're upset or stressed? How do they speak about each other to others, even when they may not be getting along? What are their strategies for spending time together despite the demands of work?

1 _____ and _____. They speak to each
other with _____. They speak about each other in
_____ terms. They spend time together by doing
_____.

2 _____ and _____. They speak to each
other with _____. They speak about each other in
_____ terms. They spend time together by doing
_____.

3 _____ and _____. They speak to each
other with _____. They speak about each other in
_____ terms. They spend time together by doing
_____.

Make Your Relationship a Priority

Within the security of a marriage, it can sometimes be easy to assume that your connection can survive without nurturance. You put your relationship on autopilot, banking on the strong foundation of love in the early married years to see you through.

But making your marriage a priority is an ongoing, active endeavor. Making your relationship a priority means intentionally strengthening your sense of teamwork. It means preparing your marriage to withstand hardship. It means saying no to people, activities, or distractions that take energy away from your marriage. And it means sharing a vision for the future that is healthy and positive, that values your individuality as much as it values your partnership. Think about your marriage in the metaphor of a bank account. This is a helpful metaphor for getting along, keeping your interactions healthy, and making your relationship a priority.

The "money" of your marriage bank is your communication, your interactions, and your repair attempts. "Depositing money" carries a positive connotation—you're infusing your marriage with love, connection, and goodwill. "Withdrawing money" carries a negative connotation—you're depleting your reserves when you or your partner use relationship poisons, hold grudges, or communicate ineffectively. An "overdraft" would feel like conflict temporarily overwhelms connection, and the solution would be to quickly move "funds" into the account by refocusing on positive interactions.

A marriage bank account that hits "bankruptcy" needs serious support and attention, hopefully leading the couple into marriage counseling for some major "financial restructuring." The goal is to prioritize your spending and saving to keep your account "in the black," to always put more money in than you take out, and to operate with deep "reserve funds" to protect your marriage from the expected and unexpected fluctuations in funds that life will bring.

ASSESS YOUR MARRIAGE "BANK ACCOUNT"

What kinds of behaviors and interactions put money in your marriage bank account?

_____

_____

_____

_____

What kinds of interactions or situations withdraw money from your bank account?

_____

_____

_____

_____

Before starting the work of this workbook, what was the state of your marriage account?

_____

_____

_____

_____

Now that you're making real progress repairing and enriching your relationship, how healthy is your current marriage bank account?

_____

_____

_____

_____

The next time you or your partner are invited to do something that would take energy away from your marriage, consider saying no to this "withdrawal." For example, you're asked to join a committee at your child's school that meets on the night of your regular date night. Or you're invited to speak at an annual conference that overlaps with your anniversary weekend. Instead of agreeing to activities that place your marriage at the bottom of the heap, say no and keep it at the top of the priority list.

Think about a period in your marriage that you'd consider "the best of times," when the "money" in your marriage bank account was abundant.

What were the circumstances of your life then?

_____

_____

_____

_____

What joys or successes were you experiencing?

_____

_____

_____

_____

What challenges were you handling well?

_____

_____

_____

_____

What resources did you have access to?

_____

_____

_____

_____

What did you appreciate most about your partner? What personality traits, strengths, and talents did your partner show that you admired and valued?

_____

_____

_____

_____

What can you replicate from that time into your present?

_____

_____

_____

_____

LOOK INTO THE FUTURE

What might be the status of your marriage bank account in the future? Take turns completing the following sentences. Remember to use the communication skills from step 1 (page 60) to share and listen.

I'm excited about _____

_____.

I'm worried about _____

_____.

I'm ready for _____

_____.

I'm curious about _____

_____.

I love _____

_____.

Look back over the discussions and exercises in this chapter. What did you learn? What are the important new ideas for you? How will you use them to strengthen your marriage?

_____

_____

_____

_____

How are you feeling? How is your partner feeling? What are the similarities and differences in how you're feeling? (See appendix A for help with identifying your feelings.)

_____

_____

_____

_____

ACTION ITEMS

Here are specific actions you can take to implement the lessons and ideas you learned in this chapter:

1 Share a personal hobby with your partner. For example, if you like to cook, register for a cooking class together. Or if your partner likes to kayak, sign up for a kayaking lesson together.
2 Volunteer together for a cause you both care about.
3 Plan an outing or date night for your partner . . . to have solo! For example, does your partner love the spa? Buy a massage package and send them off to relax. Or does your partner love a local sports team? Buy a ticket to a game and send them off to cheer.
4 Pick a code word—something silly, like _pickles_ or _monkeys_—and say it to each other a few times a day. Inside jokes and secrets can spark a sense of insular fun!

5 Refresh the photos you have hanging in your house. Print a different wedding photo, update the photos of the kids, and print your favorite selfie. The process of choosing photos reminds you of happy times together and happy times apart.

BONUS

Now that you've completed the first four steps, plan a celebration to mark the important and meaningful work you're doing to repair and enrich your marriage. What would you like to do? Plan a dinner date or go to a movie? Buy each other a present? Write each other a love letter? Spend the night in a fancy hotel? It doesn't matter what you do, but it does matter that you celebrate your progress!

BUILD TRUST

Fidelity in a marriage isn't just sexual; it's emotional, physical, psychological, and spiritual. When you trust your partner in marriage, you are saying *I can trust who you are*. It means that you respect and understand your partner's actions and decisions, that you believe your partner is reliable in their word and predictably safe in their choices. Trust is the ability to coexist peacefully with the unknown and to act with incomplete information because you've filled in the gaps with assumed knowledge that feels safe, intimate, and understandable.

Trust requires a mystical blend of intimate knowledge of another person, and a willingness to accept that another person can never fully, wholly be known. In marriage, trust is an essential ingredient for success. Breaches of trust are like holes in the bottom of a boat: Whether the water seeps in through hundreds of tiny rot spots or gushes through one gaping hole, without repair, that boat is going to sink. (But you could always decide to get on another boat together!)

The work of this chapter is intense and deeply personal. I hope you and your partner are able to use the following exercises to initiate meaningful conversation about the trust in your marriage and to address both the big and small ways trust may be undermined.

Take a moment to fill in the areas of strength and conflict from your everyday issues assessment (page 11) that will guide your focus in this step.

Step 5: Build Trust

Strengths _____ and _____

Conflicts _____ and _____

Build Trust with Time-Outs

Despite your best intentions, the train of communication will still derail. Sometimes it's a spectacular crash; other times you feel the wheels start to rattle and you know to slow down. That's what a time-out does—it slows things down so that you can both get back on the track of connection, mutual understanding, and alignment. Taking a pause from a difficult conversation is also a way to build and maintain trust in your marriage. It says to your partner, *"What we're talking about is important, but I'm having trouble listening with my heart. Trust me to take a break and come back when I'm ready."*

Here are the step-by-step Dos and Don'ts of taking a time-out:

1   Frame the need for a time-out in terms of your own experience, rather than blaming your partner.
    • DON'T blame your partner by saying something like, "You're getting really worked up. Let's take a break so you can calm down."
    • DO acknowledge the helpfulness of a time-out for yourself. For example: "I'm feeling overwhelmed. What you're saying is important, but I'm having trouble really listening to what you're saying. I need a break, and then we can try again."
2   Engage in healthy self-soothing.
    • DON'T numb or escalate (that is, don't avoid or minimize your feelings, use substances, shame or blame yourself for needing a break, complain to others, or shut down).
    • DO relax and recover. For example, meditate, take a shower or a bath, exercise or go for a walk, drink a glass of water or eat a healthy snack, write in a journal, read, or watch a funny TV show.

INTERACTING WITH EACH OTHER DURING THE TIME-OUT

You may still need to interact with each other during the break from your difficult conversation. Perhaps you need to get the kids to bed during the time-out or meet friends for brunch. How should you interact with each other during the in-between time? Remember, the time-out is meant to repair a communication derailment, not to do further damage. So it's important to be careful with your body language and words while the time-out is happening. You can be warm *and* not ready to talk about the issue at hand. You can process hurt feelings *and* not punish your partner.

- DON'T be passive-aggressive, cold, distant, or sarcastic; don't slam doors or sigh heavily.
- DO be respectful, warm, friendly, and kind; maintain small acts of affection, and smile.

3 Revisit the conversation in your mind to prepare for another try.
   - DON'T skip this step. Couples who only self-soothe but don't engage in the work of perspective taking end up rehashing the same fight over and over again. Time-outs are helpful only if you both identify ways you can do better the next time. Recovery takes active processing.
   - DO remember what is important. Couples are ready to try again for a productive conversation when they've spent the time-out actively processing what happened. What's important is that you're a team, you speak and listen with your heart, and you prevent further damage. Ask yourself questions like, "When I felt triggered, what did I think my partner was really trying to say or intending to mean? What triggered my partner? How do I imagine they felt? How can I state my needs differently so my partner can hear me? How can I convey that I understand where my partner is coming from, even if I don't agree?"

4 Try again.

- DON'T assume that because you're feeling better from the self-soothing and the active processing that you don't need to talk about the conflict. Honor the request to try again, and give yourselves the chance to get back to the original issue.
- DO return to the conversation when you're both ready. Bring a more intentional awareness of the skills you've learned, like active listening (see page 74) or Stop, Drop, Swap (see page 73). And add in some physical touching this time—remember, it's harder to argue when you're touching!

IDENTIFY YOUR TIME-OUT DOS AND DON'TS

Identify the items in the Don'ts lists that you've done in the past when you've taken a break from a difficult conversation. Write them here, and add any other unhelpful ways you've behaved in the past:

Don'ts:

_____

_____

_____

_____

These are behaviors you'll now avoid. Next, identify the items in the Dos list that you can commit to intentionally practicing instead. Write them here:

Dos:

_____

_____

_____

_____

The next time you and your partner are in the middle of a time-out, practice the behaviors on the Dos list that prevent further damage. Did they make a difference? What was hard for you about avoiding the behaviors on the Don'ts list? Did your partner notice your efforts? Did you notice your partner's efforts?

_____

_____

_____

_____

BUILDING TRUST: CARLOS AND JANELLE

Back in step 1, Carlos and Janelle had a conversation about the dishes that was full of destructive patterns of communication. Go back to page 61 and read it again, then return to this page. Here are two ways the same conversation could go, using the Dos and avoiding the Don'ts of a time-out. In the first scenario, Janelle calls for one; in the second scenario, Carlos does. (Keep your finger on page 61 so that you can flip back and forth.)

SCENARIO 1

When Carlos says, "Really? You're telling me I don't care about our home? I help you ALL THE TIME!" here's how the conversation goes instead:

JANELLE: *Wow. I need a break. I can feel my heart rate rising, and I don't want to say something I don't mean. I think I'm going to get out of the apartment for a few minutes.*

CARLOS: *Are you going to go for a walk?*

JANELLE: *Yeah.*

CARLOS: *Okay, see you when you get back.*

Later, when Janelle gets back:

> JANELLE: *Come sit with me on the couch? Okay, so I think what triggered me was your comment about "I don't think it's so bad." When I look around, I see so many things that could be put away or cleaned up. It's frustrating to me when you look around and don't see the same things. I do acknowledge that you help. And I appreciate the things you do...*

SCENARIO 2

When Janelle says, "This drives me crazy! I can't be the only one who cares about our home!" here's how the conversation goes instead:

> CARLOS: *Nope. Not going to go there with you. Telling me I don't care is a trigger for me. I want to help you today, and I will. But I need to take a break first. I'm going to take a quick shower.*

Later:

> CARLOS: *Yeah... so our shower is pretty disgusting. You're totally right that we need to clean the bathrooms today. I'm sorry I started arguing with you about the apartment. I was feeling lazy and got defensive when you called the mess my "crap"...*

PRACTICE TIME-OUTS

The next time a conversation starts to derail, practice taking a time-out. Then check in with yourself by asking the following questions:

Which step was the hardest for me to do?

_____

_____

_____

_____

How did we treat each other during the time-out?

_____

_____

_____

_____

How can we improve our use of the time-out strategy to repair and enrich our connection?

_____

_____

_____

_____

Do we feel closer and more trusting after taking a time-out?

_____

_____

_____

_____

Betrayals

Betrayals in a marriage take many forms, from affairs to secrets to lies. At its core, a betrayal is a form of disloyalty—an indication that something or someone else has taken priority, preference, or value over the partnership. Like the relationship poisons discussed on page 17, betrayal in a marriage is toxic because it signals violations of marriage values like mutuality, respect, and teamwork. Two of the most common forms of betrayal in marriage, besides sexual betrayals, are secrets and lies.

SECRETS

Secrets in a marriage can take different forms—perhaps you've started withholding information to avoid a conflict, like when you use cash to pay for something so there isn't a credit card trail. Or perhaps you're keeping secrets from your partner because you're ashamed of the truth (or what your partner would think about your truth), like when you bought a pack of cigarettes even though you're trying to quit and your partner would be disappointed.

Marriage asks us to be vulnerable and open with our partner, and requires us to do our part to create the emotionally safe environment that facilitates such sharing. It asks of one another, "Share your true self with me."

EXPLORE PAST SECRETS

Think about how secrets were handled in your family growing up, and how they were handled in your early dating relationships.

Were you implicitly expected or explicitly asked to keep secrets from other people in your family? How did that feel? Were the secrets ever exposed?

_____

_____

_____

_____

Were you implicitly expected or explicitly asked to keep secrets from other people to protect your partner or yourself? How did that feel? Were the secrets ever exposed?

_____

_____

_____

_____

Think about a secret you've never told your partner before. Perhaps it's a story or experience from your childhood or early dating relationships, perhaps it's a dream you have for the future, or perhaps it's a secret fear. Use the communication skills from step 1 (page 60) to share a secret with your partner to deepen intimacy and build trust. How did that feel?

_____

_____

_____

_____

LIES

Consistency and honesty are two very important values in a partnership. To build lives together, you need to know that your partner will do what they say and say what they mean, and vice versa. Intentional deception quickly undermines trust in a marriage, no matter if the lies are "white" or "whoppers." Similar to why we might keep a secret from our partner, a lie can be a way to avoid confrontation. "I didn't tell you because I knew you'd get upset—just like you're doing now!" But lying only compounds the injury; one wound is the difficult truth itself, and the other is the deception that hid that truth. I often hear from my clients, even those dealing with a betrayal on the level of an affair, that the lying hurts more than the actions.

8 DESTRUCTIVE HABITS AND 8 WELLNESS HABITS

Destructive behaviors undermine trust in a marriage, especially when partners have shared concerns about unhealthy behavior and changes are not made. Of course, we all have habits of behavior or thinking that could be categorized as addictive or destructive, as well as habits that signify our commitment to health and wellness. But it's not always so clear-cut—a potentially addictive or destructive habit can be healthy in moderation or within safe boundaries, and obsessive or excessive health and wellness habits can become destructive. Review the following destructive habits and wellness habits:

Destructive Habits	Wellness Habits
Aggressive driving	Nutrition
Alcohol/Drugs	Active lifestyle
Caffeine	Hygiene
Extreme exercise	Sleep
Fast food	Social support
Pessimism	Preventive health care
Sexually explicit material	Sunscreen
Sugar	Optimism

IDENTIFY YOUR HABITS

In the worksheet below, fill in the habits you are struggling with, the ones you are proud of, those you may be doing in excess, and those you aren't doing enough of. If you are sharing your answers with your partner, remember to use the skills of healthy communication from step 1 (page 60).

Struggling with

_____

_____

_____

_____

Proud of

_____

_____

_____

_____

May be doing to excess

_____

_____

_____

_____

Want to do more of

_____

_____

_____

_____

TELL A TRUTH

Think about something you've lied to your partner about. Perhaps it's a story you left an important detail out of or an exaggeration that has become normalized, or perhaps it's a lie you've been telling yourself, too. Use the communication skills from step 1 (page 60) to tell the truth to your partner to deepen intimacy and build trust. How did that feel?

_____

_____

_____

_____

BUILDING TRUST: JOSH AND HEATHER

After the third night in a row that Josh didn't come home from work until one in the morning, Heather was furious. The kind of furious that is icy cold and dangerously calm. The next evening, when he called to tell her he'd be late again, she decided to find out what was really going on. She called a neighbor to watch the kids and drove to his work.

When she burst into his office, she saw Josh with his feet on his desk, takeout Chinese in one hand and an open beer in the other. Josh watched the emotions flash across her face: first rage, then confusion, then deep hurt. She started to cry.

Here are snippets of the conversation that came next:

HEATHER: *How could you lie to me? I support your work, I understand sometimes you have to be here late and I'm on my own with the kids. But takeout and beers? I'm devastated.*

JOSH: *I'm so sorry, Heather. I didn't know how to tell you that I'm really struggling as a dad right now. I feel powerless at home, and I figured I'd just avoid the whole thing.*

HEATHER: *You've been avoiding us? Me?*

JOSH: *There's no space for me at home.*

Heather left the office, needing a time-out from their conversation and what she had learned. Josh quickly followed her home. They recognized the significant work ahead to rebuild trust and partnership.

SELF-SOOTHING AFTER BETRAYAL

Betrayals in marriage can feel like traumas; they can deeply wound our sense of emotional safety and disrupt our sense of the world as predictable and stable. And often, betrayal in a marriage becomes instantly linked to painful experiences from previous relationships—because similar emotional signatures trigger similar emotional responses.

After the trauma of a relationship betrayal, your brain goes into fight-or-flight mode. You are flooded with stress hormones, your body is ready to fight or flee, and where there are links to past traumas, your emotional experience is intensified by those memories. Self-soothing activates the parts of our brain that calm us, ground us in the present, and reduce the terror. Here are a few ways to self-soothe:

- Listen to classical or meditative music.
- Practice deep breathing.
- Engage in gentle touch, such as petting your cat or dog, submerging in water, or using a weighted blanket.
- Spend time in nature, walking or watching, and connecting to the earth.

The best self-soothing behaviors are the activities that make you feel safe, peaceful, and calm. You may need to soothe for hours or for days, but no matter what, I want you to remember that you are capable of coping and, eventually, of trusting and feeling joy again.

AFTER AN AFFAIR

Affairs are always hurtful in a marriage, but they are not necessarily traumatic. Yes, there will be intense distress, but an affair mustn't always result in irreparable damage. Wherever there is deep suffering, there is the potential for a kind of wake-up that is a rebirth.

When your mind-set gets entrenched in the belief that your partner has rejected you, an affair turns you into a victim. When you believe that there is something wrong with you, it is difficult to rebuild closeness and redefine love. Instead, experiencing infidelity as a *very* unwelcome opportunity to grow, change, and learn about each other places you in the role of resilient conqueror. Intimacy is rediscovered, leaps of faith land you in safe territory, and your marriage is reborn.

People are capable of experiencing difficult circumstances—a terrible accident, a malignant tumor, a house that burns down—and overcoming them with strength, courage, and growth. But don't misunderstand me: Just as I would never, ever wish those experiences upon anyone, I do not wish for an affair to happen for your marriage to come back to life. I only maintain that it *is* possible for a second marriage, to the same person, to emerge after an affair.

Although there are many excellent resources and self-help books that can help couples recover after an affair, I strongly recommend seeking the assistance of a qualified marriage-counseling specialist. In my practice, affair recovery includes the following conversations:

- Reframing the affair as a marital crisis, rather than as a personal crisis
- Processing the full range of intense emotions as they cycle: rage, confusion, hurt, jealousy, numbing, avoidance, remorse, and so on
- Exploring the factors that created the vulnerability for an affair, factors that both partners contributed to, and what was lost in the marriage before the affair
- Deciding the extent to which details about the affair will be disclosed, and preparing for what that disclosure will mean
- Practicing behaviors that cultivate trust, moving from surveillance and hyper-vigilance to openness and vulnerability

These are difficult conversations to have on your own—and you don't have to. You can seek and find a qualified marriage-counseling specialist to help you and your partner if you're struggling after an affair.

BUILDING TRUST: BETH AND MEI-LIN

Beth and Mei-Lin's relationship started as an affair—Beth was in a relationship with Clara when she met Mei-Lin at a party. She cheated on Clara with Mei-Lin for two weeks before she ended the relationship with Clara.

"At first, I didn't know she was dating someone else," says Mei-Lin. "When she told me about Clara after she ended it with her, I was a wreck. I felt confused and hurt that she would lie to me, that she would do that to another partner."

Beth says: "I knew what I was doing was wrong, but I . . ."

"There are no 'but's. It was wrong."

"Right. I know."

When Beth and Mei-Lin were ready to commit to each other five years ago during a private ceremony, they decided to go to couples counseling first. "I wanted to make sure we were okay, that Mei-Lin trusted me. And if she was still feeling uneasy about whether I'd ever cheat on her, like I did with Clara, I wanted to learn how to earn her trust," says Beth.

"Beth isn't a 'therapy person,' so asking her to go with me was huge. And it was really helpful. I don't think we could have felt so confident committing to each other without doing the work with our therapist first," says Mei-Lin.

"And we're going to go back! I figure, it can't hurt to have a tune-up before the wedding, right, Mei-Lin?"

Forgiveness: Rebuild Trust from the Ground Up

I'd like to start this section on forgiveness by offering you my hope, a sincere wish from my therapist heart: May we all do the hard, transformative, and courageous work to process the injuries done to us so that we live our lives with vitality, freedom, and joy.

Most of us carry mistaken assumptions about what forgiveness is—what it means, who gives it, and what happens afterward. So let's do some more myth busting!

Myth: There is no choice other than to forgive or not forgive.

Reality: Forgiveness should be conceptualized as a continuum of choices, each with risks and benefits. Forgiveness isn't all or nothing.

Myth: Forgiveness is unconditional.

Reality: Approaching forgiveness as a transaction rather than a gift enables us to maintain a sense of integrity and self-worth. Forgiveness is earned.

Myth: Forgiveness comes easily and naturally . . . if we just let it flow.

Reality: Western culture does little to teach us in explicit and concrete ways how to navigate the complicated waters of forgiveness—especially when the person who hurt us isn't sorry. Forgiveness takes time and effort.

Okay, so if we know what forgiveness is *not*—a binary, unconditional choice that comes naturally—then we know what forgiveness *is*: an intimate dance with the person who hurt you, a dance that must be learned and is best when earned.

WHEN FORGIVENESS COMES TOO EASILY

Be wary of an urge to quickly forgive. When forgiveness is premature, superficial, and unilateral, it is not healing. When forgiveness comes too easily, there is no processing of emotion and no coming to terms with the injury. For example, "I'm fine. It's okay. Whatever, I don't want to talk about it. Let's just move on."

When you're too quick to smooth things over and move on, you take away the opportunity for your partner to learn from their mistakes and make different choices in the future. How can your partner apologize for something you minimize?

One strategy is to give voice to the injury that happened. Using the skills you learned in step 1, tell your partner how you felt when the situation happened, and explain what they can do to repair the damage. Assertively sharing your perspective and experience creates the opportunity for your partner to take responsibility for the hurt they caused and for forgiveness to be earned. How did that go?

_____

_____

_____

_____

WHEN FORGIVENESS IS SUPPRESSED

Be wary of an urge to refuse to forgive. When forgiveness is rigidly withheld to be punishing or retaliatory, it is not healing. When forgiveness is suppressed, you're stuck stewing in rage and nonnegotiable anger. You're stuck clinging to indignation and contempt. For example, "No matter what you say or do to repent, I will never stop making you pay for the hurt you have caused."

Sometimes, when you're blinded by your hurt, it's hard to see the positive things your partner is doing to rebuild trust. Or maybe you do see the ways they're trying to repair, but you don't want them to have weight or meaning. How can you open yourself up to healing, to absorbing the love your partner is trying to give?

For the next few days, look to strangers to remind you of love and kindness existing in all kinds of relationships. Look for people being nice to each other, like friends enjoying a meal or someone holding a door open for a mom with a stroller. Let the kindness you witness among strangers reorient you to being open to kindness in your marriage, to being touched by it. Write down some of those kindnesses you witnessed here:

_____

_____

_____

_____

When your heart is full of witnessing love among others, turn back to witnessing love in the most intimate person in your life—your partner.

WHEN YOUR PARTNER REFUSES TO PARTICIPATE IN FORGIVENESS

It is a difficult position to be in when you're dealing with a partner who refuses to help heal their damage or be involved in earning your forgiveness. But whether or not they participate, the choice to accept the reality of your partner's avoidance can be empowering, life affirming, and personally healing.

You decide for yourself how to transcend the injury, to make peace with what happened, and to free yourself from its burden. For example, "I've come to understand that you are unwilling to acknowledge what you did to me. I don't wish you harm, but I also need boundaries in my life with you to protect myself from further damage. I am worthy of love, and I give it to myself. I have honored my pain, and I am free of it."

Accepting that your partner is unwilling or unable to participate in the forgiveness process is a difficult thing to do. Focusing on self-care behaviors grounds you in self-love and gives you the strength to set boundaries and move on with your life.

Establish a ritual of self-love. Think of one behavior, however simple or complex, that you can do on a regular basis that signifies your commitment to take care of your soul and yourself. Perhaps it's a positive affirmation you repeat to yourself every time you're stopped at a red light: "I am a person of worth. I am worthy of love." Or perhaps it's a weekly run through the park or a yoga class that sweats out the negative feelings that build up in your heart. Write it here and then make a commitment to yourself to do it.

_____

_____

_____

_____

FORGIVENESS GENUINELY EARNED AND SINCERELY GIVEN

When forgiveness is genuinely earned and sincerely given, it is interpersonal, contextual, and extraordinary. With heartfelt participation, your partner who hurt you works hard to earn forgiveness through generous acts of repentance. At the same time, you work hard to let go of resentment to allow the damage to be healed. It's an exchange, a conversation, that goes something like this:

PARTNER 1: *"I will bear witness to the pain I caused, and I will apologize genuinely and nondefensively. I will seek to understand my behavior, and I will earn your trust. I will forgive myself, as you work to forgive me, so that I make a sincere attempt toward atonement."*

PARTNER 2: *"I will help you understand the full sweep of my emotions without drowning in my pain. I will create opportunities for you to make good on your attempts to repent so that I can heal. I will reengage in a life with you safely and on new terms. I will not dwell in the past but will learn to trust you in the present."*

As you learned in step 1, attunement and alignment are the emotional stances that build trust and restore safety. When you're attuned to your partner, you've given up your need to be right, your need to be a wounded victim, and your resistance to recovery.

Aligning with your partner requires you to meet each other in a spirit of shared, mutual support. Each of you is able to share feelings and needs, each of you is able to listen to your partner's words, and together you are able to deepen your connection by understanding each other's perspective and experience. Together, you are able to repair emotional damage and build trust by compromising, expressing affection, setting boundaries, taking responsibility, seeking to understand, and prioritizing *we*.

DISCUSS RESTORING TRUST AND SAFETY

Are you ready to meet each other in the emotional stances of attunement and alignment? Why or why not? If not, what do you think still needs to happen? Use the skills you learned in step 1 (page 60) to have a conversation about restoring trust and safety to your marriage.

_____

_____

_____

_____

THREE LEVELS OF GOOD APOLOGIES

It's difficult to genuinely apologize! Apologizing is a vulnerable and humbling position—and that can be difficult for most people. We have much more experience with defensiveness or explanation than we do with crafting good apologies. I teach couples in my practice about apologies by separating different kinds of apologies into three levels:

LEVEL 1

Saying "I'm sorry" when neither of you is at fault but you want to acknowledge your partner's pain, frustration, or sadness. Level 1 apologies usually require little effort to say, but they are meaningful because you are communicating that you care. For example:

> Linda had a tough interview with the community college mathematics faculty chair. Tim says, "I'm sorry, sweetheart. I know how hard you prepared for that meeting. It sucks the chair was dismissive of your syllabus recommendations."

LEVEL 2

Saying "I'm sorry" when you are at fault, when you need to apologize for bad behavior, hurt feelings, or misunderstandings. Level 2 apologies require some forethought and preparation to make sure you're communicating that you understand the impact of your behavior on your partner and take responsibility for your role. Sometimes Level 2 apologies are lightened by humor. For example:

> Linda is upset that she had to attend a family wedding without her husband. Tim says, "I'm sorry I missed the wedding. I know it was difficult for you to be there without me and answer questions about my absence. I should have double-checked the dates of my work conference before agreeing to go. At least we got them a really nice wedding present, right? You know I'm only kidding—I promise I'll think of a way to make it up to your family and to you."

LEVEL 3

Saying "I'm sorry" when you have deep regret for something happening that you caused or something that didn't happen because you didn't act. Level 3 apologies require humility, vulnerability, and patience—sometimes the receiver needs time to heal before accepting. And sometimes the circumstances requiring a Level 3 apology from one partner require some kind of apology from the other as well, even if not at the same level. For example:

Tim bought Linda a birthday gift that she didn't like, and she lied about returning it when confronted by Tim, who already knew the truth.

LINDA SAYS: *"I'm sorry I returned the present and then lied about whether I still had it. I was trying to avoid telling you I didn't like it, but I ended up making things so much worse. I understand that my lie was more hurtful to you than not liking the present. It was selfish of me to put avoiding my discomfort before your right to know the truth. Honesty is important to me in our marriage, and I recognize that I undermined your trust by lying."*

TIM REPLIES: *"And I'm sorry I snooped to see if you still had the gift. I already knew you hadn't kept the present, so I shouldn't have set you up. It wasn't fair to ask you a question I already knew the answer to."*

PRACTICE APOLOGIZING AT ALL THREE LEVELS

The next time you or your partner needs to apologize, name the level—actually say to each other, "That was a Level 1 apology" or "I'm about to try for a Level 3 apology, so please bear with me." Labeling the level will increase your awareness of what to include. How did that go?

_____

_____

_____

_____

Look back over the discussions and exercises in this chapter. What did you learn? What are the important new ideas for you? How will you use them to strengthen your marriage?

_____

_____

_____

_____

How are you feeling? How is your partner feeling? What are the similarities and differences in how you're feeling? (See appendix A for help with identifying your feelings.)

_____

_____

_____

_____

ACTION ITEM

Because this chapter is so deeply personal, there is only one in-depth action item, and I call it "The ABCs of Building Trust." It will help you implement the lessons and ideas you learned in this chapter. Here are the steps:

1 Build trust by using the alphabet as prompts for loving conversation. First, flip back to step 1 and remind yourselves of the skills of assertive heart speaking (page 66).
2 Write each letter of the alphabet on a blank page, cut out all the letters, and fold each letter in half. Put the letters in a bowl or jar and place it in your bedroom.
3 Each night before you go to bed for the next 13 nights, each of you will choose a letter from the container. (If you and your partner don't go to bed at the same time, set aside another point in your evening routines instead.)

4 Use the letter you choose as your prompt to share a loving thought, a happy memory, a gratitude message, a compliment, or admirable qualities that start with your letter. You can each build on the other's share, or you can take things in your own direction.

5 Keep your "speeches" short and sweet. Allow them to infuse your wounded hearts with love and tenderness. If you feel up to it, kiss at the end when both of you have shared.

Here's an example from Josh and Heather to get you started:

JOSH *chooses Z: "I remember last summer when you were pregnant with Lucy, we took Mason to the zoo. You must have been so hot, and we walked and walked. Mason and I both kinda lost it, but I don't remember you complaining once. I appreciate that you always try really hard to make our rare family days special."*

HEATHER *chooses S: "I remember that day too! You scooped Mason up and put him up on your shoulders so he could get a better view of the elephants. You were pointing and he was looking and you were holding on to each other. I love that image of my two boys. I remember thinking, I can't wait to have another baby with this amazing dad."*

JOSH: *"'Amazing dad'—I don't often feel that way. It feels good to hear you say that."*

HEATHER: *"You really are, Josh."*

REVISIT FAMILY

Family. Let's all let out a collective sigh. What is it about family that we simultaneously yearn for and can't wait to get away from? How can our parents drive us crazy one minute and then make us feel like we belong the next? And how the heck did your partner emerge so normal(ish) from a family like . . . that?

Most of us can say that our family members mean well, but that doesn't mean they don't put enormous strain on a marriage. In this step, we're going to revisit your families of origin by examining your relationships with your parents and your partner's parents. We're also going to consider the role that children play in your marriage, your parenting styles, and how you balance parenthood with partnership. My hope is that you'll finish the chapter with a deeper understanding of your family stressors, and with new strategies for how to deal with them.

Take a moment to fill in the areas of strength and conflict from your everyday issues assessment (page 11) that will guide your focus in this step.

Step 6: Revisit Family

Strengths _____ and _____

Conflicts _____ and _____

Family Relationships

In chapter 2, we journeyed back in time to discover the ways your family of origin and childhood experiences have influenced your life and your relationships. In this step, we're going to explore how family relationships are affecting your marriage now. Before you start the work of this step, it may be helpful to flip back to chapter 2 and review the exercises. How did you draw your family aquarium? How do your childhood experiences shape your marriage now?

INFLUENCE FROM PARENTS AND IN-LAWS

As we grow up from children to adults, relationships with our parents shift. Let's look at the relationships you have with your parents and in-laws. Many newlywed and married couples in my practice describe the joys and challenges of staying connected with parents. The following exercises will help you identify your preferences for accepting their influence, the ways their help may come with strings attached, and how fundamental family therapy concepts like relationship triangles and reactivity can help explain the ways family shapes our emotional worlds.

ASSESS YOUR COMFORT LEVEL

Answer True or False to the following statements in parts A and B:

PART A: YOUR PARENTS

> T / F *I seek guidance from my parents while making decisions.*
>
> T / F *I care about what my parents think of my choices.*
>
> T / F *I value time with my parents.*
>
> T / F *I share personal details with my parents about my life and relationship.*
>
> T / F *I allow my parents to help me financially.*

T / F *I seek out guidance from my in-laws while making decisions.*

T / F *I care about what my in-laws think of my choices.*

T / F *I value time with my in-laws.*

T / F *I share personal details with my in-laws about my life and relationship.*

T / F *I allow my in-laws to help me financially.*

If you answer mostly True (for either part A, part B, or both), you tend to be comfortable accepting influence from your parents and/or from your in-laws. The boundaries are flexible and permeable—information, money, time, and advice flow freely between you.

If you answered mostly False (for either part A, part B, or both), you are not comfortable accepting influence from your parents and/or from your in-laws. The boundaries are rigid and firm—information, money, time, and advice are resisted between you.

COMPARE COMFORT LEVELS

Here is Carlos's reaction after completing the quizzes with Janelle:

Carlos was a little surprised to find out that Janelle doesn't feel comfortable accepting influence from his parents, just like he doesn't. "I knew we didn't agree about your parents, but I thought we'd be arguing about my parents, too," says Carlos. "I figured you've been upset that they're not more involved in our life like your parents are."

"Heck no!" says Janelle. "I've got more than enough to manage with my own family. I'd rather not have your crazy mom (no offense) all up in our business, too!"

"None taken," Carlos says with a chuckle. "Remember how insane it was at our wedding? My mom was doing tequila shots with my aunts and cousins and shouting at the DJ in Spanish."

Compare answers with your partner.

Does your comfort level with your parents match your partner's comfort level with your parents (their in-laws), and vice versa? _____

Is your comfort level with accepting influence the same for your parents and your in-laws? _____

How do similarities or differences between you and your partner strengthen your partnership? How do they cause problems? _____

Where would you like to make changes in accepting more or less influence from your parents and from your partner's parents? _____

Were you surprised by your or your partner's answers to the questions in this exercise?

_____

_____

_____

_____

QUID PRO QUOS

The phrase *quid pro quo* means "this for that." When it comes to parental or family involvement in your lives as a married couple, there are often expectations about what will come in return. These bargains may be explicit, or they may be simply understood. Sure, your mother-in-law is willing to babysit for you, but she expects an invitation to dinner at your house in return. Sure, your father is willing to loan you and your partner money for a car repair, but he expects to be thanked profusely for his generosity.

Fill in the blanks and discuss with your partner. Here are two examples, from Mei-Lin and Beth, to get you started:

MEI-LIN SAYS: *If my sister offers to help by cat sitting when we're on vacation, the expectation is that we'll stock up on her favorite foods and leave her money to get groceries. How does this usually go for us? Not too badly, I guess. I'd rather have her watch the cats than someone we hire whom we don't know. Seems like a small price to pay.*

BETH SAYS: *If my dad offers to help by paying for part of the wedding, the expectation is that he'll get recognition, like getting to make a speech at dinner, and that he'll get to bring "the girlfriend." How does this usually go for us? Well, it hasn't happened yet, but I'm not interested in her being at my wedding. So I'd rather not take the money.*

If my _____ offers help by

_____,

the expectation is that _____

_____.

How does this usually go for us? _____

_____

If my _____ offers help by

_____,

the expectation is that _____

_____.

How does this usually go for us? _____

_____

RELATIONSHIP TRIANGLES

A relationship triangle is a natural human response to anxiety or conflict in a relationship. When two people feel distant, uncomfortable, angry, or hurt with one another, a third person (or sometimes, a situation, like going to work) gets triangled in to balance the emotional intensity. Sometimes that person is within the family system, like a child or parent, and other times that person is outside, like an affair or best friend. Here are a few common examples:

- A husband and wife feel disconnected, and the wife confides in her neighbor.
- A husband and his mother are very close, and the mother shuns the wife.
- A mother and daughter are very close, and the father feels like he has to compete for his wife's attention.

Understanding and identifying triangles within relationships is an advanced skill. Here are detailed examples from Carlos and Janelle and Josh and Heather to help you better understand how triangles operate in family relationships:

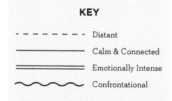

KEY

- - - - - - - Distant
——————— Calm & Connected
═══════════ Emotionally Intense
∿∿∿∿∿∿ Confrontational

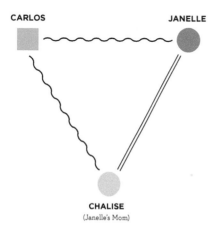

CARLOS **JANELLE**

CHALISE
(Janelle's Mom)

Carlos has been offered a job as a school administrator a few counties away. He and Janelle have been arguing about whether to move for weeks. Janelle wants to stay close to her parents; Carlos wants the opportunity to grow in his career. Janelle's mom doesn't want her only daughter to move away either, and she starts emailing Carlos to let him know. Carlos calls her to tell her to stop meddling in his marriage, which only results in another screaming match between him and Janelle.

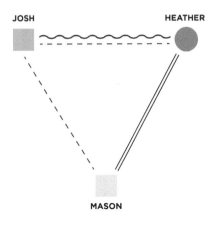

JOSH   HEATHER

MASON

When Mason was born, Heather experienced postpartum depression and made Josh out to be her enemy. She was convinced he didn't help her with the baby or the housework enough, and her moods were unpredictable. Josh responded to Heather's criticism and negativity with defensiveness and distance. Heather sought comfort in taking care of Mason, snuggling with him and tending to his every need. It felt good to be needed and loved. Josh felt shut out from caring for Mason, which only perpetuated Heather's perception that Josh didn't help her.

DRAW THE TRIANGLES IN YOUR FAMILY

In the space provided, draw a triangle, and on each point, write in the names that make up your relationship triangle. Draw and label as many triangles as are needed to illustrate all the triangles in your family. What do you notice?

It's difficult work to make the changes necessary to rebalance triangled relationships—to shift behavior, perspective, and attitudes. What if Carlos could relate to his mother-in-law calmly, understanding her fear of losing her daughter? What if Heather could invite Josh into her bond with Mason, encouraging his competence as a new father?

What can you do to shift your position in the triangles in your marriage or family?

_____

_____

_____

5 WAYS TO MANAGE IN-LAW INTERFERENCE

1   Communicate clearly, directly, and in a timely manner. Don't let problems linger or fester. Don't share concerns through your partner or another family member. And don't beat around the bush—remember, assertive communication is healthy communication!

2   Never put your partner in a position to have to choose between your partnership and their family. Efforts to accommodate your in-laws with respect and kindness strengthen your marriage because they support your partner. Just like it feels good when your partner accommodates your parents (their in-laws), these efforts are reciprocal.

3   Establish boundaries and expectations with your partner ahead of time and stick to them. Decide whether you'll accept loans, how involved the grandparents will be in your parenting decisions, and which family rules can slide when Grandma and Grandpa are visiting.

4   Consider maintaining a "no houseguest" policy. When family members are in town to visit, they stay at a nearby hotel or rental property. Use the time in the morning before they arrive at your house and in the evening after they leave to recharge as a couple.

5   Be yourself. Don't try to meet their expectations of you if it wouldn't be genuine.

REACTIVITY

Many problems in family relationships stem from *reactivity*, or responding to a situation or person with rigid thinking and intense emotions. Reactivity gives us a very narrow lens through which we make assumptions, draw opinions, and observe others. It prevents us from perspective taking—seeing more than one side of an issue, seeing our own part in an issue, and being able to speak and listen from the heart.

Reactivity is an automatic response; like a trigger, it fires quickly. The antidotes to reactivity are thinking, questioning, and pausing, and then speaking from your heart and sharing your values and needs. Asking questions out loud, with genuine curiosity, helps you see the situation within its larger context, allows you to reflect on what has happened, and encourages vulnerability from yourself and from others.

IDENTIFY YOUR TRIGGERS

Think about a recent incident when you responded with reactivity or jumped to a conclusion. What were your triggers in that situation?

_____

_____

_____

_____

How did your body react in that situation—with a knot in your stomach or heat traveling up your neck? What did you do to relax and "come down" from that reaction?

_____

_____

_____

_____

Can you imagine another way you could have responded to avoid being reactive?

_____

_____

_____

_____

Children and Parenting

For many couples, parenting children together brings joy and teamwork to the marriage. But for many others, parenting is just another area of disagreement. Whether you're new parents or your children are growing up, let's explore several important dimensions of parenting and how it affects you as a couple.

TRANSITION TO PARENTHOOD

The transition from a marriage of two to a family of three (or more, if you've having multiples) is one of the most difficult for couples to make. You're adding an entirely new set of roles, expectations, behaviors, and experiences to your life—now you're a partner *and* a parent. One of the hardest parts of this transition can be how gendered it is. Especially for couples today, who tend to prefer egalitarian marriage, the realities of pregnancy, childbirth, and postpartum transform a mostly gender-neutral partnership into rigid slots of "mother" and "father." Let's hear from Carlos and Linda on this topic:

CARLOS SAYS: *"Kids are really important to me; I've always known I would be a dad, so I'm concerned about our ability to get pregnant. An initial fertility consult was disheartening. It's hard sometimes to balance my confidence that we'll figure it out with my empathy for her fears—I understand that when the doctor talks about her uterus and her ovulation and her family history, she internalizes herself as the problem. But no matter what else we fight about, we don't fight about wanting babies together."*

LINDA SAYS: *"After having the two boys, we thought our family was complete. Then, when Anthony was six and Michael was four, we unexpectedly got pregnant again. At first I was conflicted—I was happy and grateful, but I wasn't in baby mode anymore. When I miscarried at 11 weeks, we were both devastated. It took us a while, but we realized that within our grief was a sincere desire to grow our family. So we decided to pursue adoption, and that's how Sabrina came into our lives."*

IF YOU ARE NOT YET PARENTS

What are your expectations of what conception, pregnancy, childbirth, and postpartum life will be like?

_____

_____

_____

_____

How do you imagine you'll respond (both individually and as a couple) to infertility, a challenging pregnancy, a birth that doesn't go according to plan, or postpartum depression/anxiety?

_____

_____

_____

_____

How will you remain connected as partners through your different roles, gendered or otherwise, during the process of becoming parents?

_____

_____

_____

_____

Were your expectations of conception, pregnancy, childbirth, and postpartum life met, exceeded, or thwarted?

_____

_____

_____

_____

How did you cope (both individually and as a couple) if you encountered infertility, a challenging pregnancy, a birth that didn't go according to plan, or postpartum depression/anxiety?

_____

_____

_____

_____

How did you remain connected as partners through your different roles, gendered or otherwise, during the process of becoming parents?

_____

_____

_____

_____

ATTACHMENT STYLES

Attachment is the idea that all humans—children and adults—need connection and belonging in order to survive and thrive. As adults, our attachment style influences our vulnerability and our protectiveness. Through attachments with parents, children make meaning of experiences and emotions. Generally, there are three attachment styles:

Anxious: People with anxious attachment are preoccupied with closeness and seek it at all costs. They fear abandonment, they worry they aren't worthy of love, and they set aside their needs to meet the needs of others. I'm not okay without you, so you can't ever leave me.

Avoidant: People with avoidant attachment are disconnected from intimacy and avoid vulnerability. They are quick to find fault in others, they increase distance to counteract closeness, and they may be perceived as sabotaging relationships. I'm fine without you, so you can leave and I won't care.

Secure: People with secure attachment are comfortably balanced between intimacy and closeness, and independence and distance. They ask for what they need while attending to others' needs, they avoid games or manipulations to maintain relationships, and they accept themselves and others as whole people. I feel safe being close to you; I love you and I love myself.

Differences in attachment styles are a common underpinning of conflict for partners who are also parents. Whether one style resonates more than the others, or you can think of ways you exhibit all three, exploring how attachment affects your marriage is a helpful way to deepen understanding of your—and your partner's—parenting.

EXPLORE ATTACHMENT DIFFERENCES

If you tend to be anxious, can you recognize ways you may be drawn into your children's world to meet your need for closeness at the expense of your partner?

_____

_____

_____

_____

If you tend to be avoidant, can you recognize ways you may abdicate your role as co-parent to meet your need for independence at the expense of your partner?

_____

_____

_____

_____

How do differences or similarities between your attachment styles contribute to problems in your marriage or your parenting?

_____

_____

_____

_____

PARENTING STYLES

It's not uncommon for partners to parent with different styles. You grew up in different families, and you play different roles in your children's lives. And it's not uncommon for these differences to cause conflict between you. First, let's explore your parenting styles and then let's learn a communication trick for handling style differences.

The grid in the next exercise has two axes. One is a spectrum of your style of connection to your children, from a warm and nurturing approach to a more neutral and inattentive approach. The other is a spectrum of your style of influencing your children, from fostering autonomy and independence in your child to using authority and control to manage behavior.

Mark an X within the grid where your parenting style lands now, and have your partner do the same in a different color. Then, mark where your ideal parenting style would be as a couple.

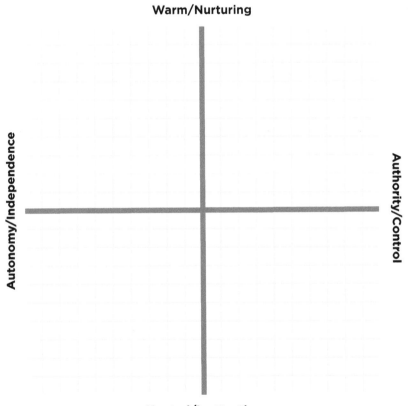

How far away are you from your partner now?

_____

_____

_____

_____

How far away are you now from where you want to be as a couple?

_____

_____

_____

_____

Do your answers surprise you? Are you more similar or more dissimilar than you expected?

_____

_____

_____

_____

MANAGE PARENTING DIFFERENCES

Differences in parenting style often mean differences in parenting behavior. And when these differences cause conflict, the solution is in your communication. So instead of getting frustrated or feeling undermined by your partner, here's a helpful trick: view the situation as if you were watching a foreign film. The subtitles help you understand what the parenting difference means and clues for what to do about it. Here is an example from Josh and Heather and their son Mason to help you get started:

The Scene: *Mason is helping make brownies; his stirring is making a mess of his clothes and the counter. Chocolate batter is everywhere.*

The Action/Dialogue: *Heather snaps at Mason, "Stop that! If you can't be more careful, I'm going to take away your tablet." Mason starts crying. Josh says, "It's okay, Mason. It's hard to stir carefully! Next time you can help clean up."*

The Subtitles: *Heather: The mess is stressing me out. I'm trying to control his behavior through threat of negative consequences.*

The Subtitles: *Josh: I expected a mess, so I'm not stressed. I'm trying to foster his autonomy and teach natural consequences.*

The Resolution: *Josh and Heather take a break to communicate their subtitles. Heather suggests that Josh should take over in the kitchen, since he feels calmer and more connected to Mason in the moment.*

The Scene: _____

_____

_____

The Action/Dialogue: _____

sees/hears: _____

_____

_____

The Subtitles: Partner 1: _____

_____

_____

The Subtitles: Partner 2: _____

_____

_____

The Resolution: _____

_____

_____

How does awareness of the subtitles help you understand your partner's parenting choices?

_____

_____

_____

_____

How does this awareness help you decide as a team how to resolve differences in your approach?

_____

_____

_____

_____

KEEPING MARRIAGE A PRIORITY

On an airplane, you are always advised to put your own oxygen mask on before helping your child put on theirs. This is a good analogy for why you must keep your marriage a priority over the children. Your marriage "mask" goes on first so you can respond well as a team to your children's needs. This means prioritizing date nights, taking some child-free vacations, and remembering that you are a partner at the same time that you're a parent.

ASSESS PRIORITIES

In the midst of parenting demands, how well are you doing with keeping your marriage a priority?

_____

_____

_____

_____

In what ways do your children currently come before your marriage?

_____

_____

_____

_____

What are you modeling for your children with regard to where your marriage falls on your priority list?

_____

_____

_____

_____

Look back over the discussions and exercises in this chapter. What did you learn? What are the important new ideas for you? How will you use them to strengthen your marriage?

_____

_____

_____

_____

How are you feeling? How is your partner feeling? What are the similarities and differences in how you're feeling? (See appendix A for help with identifying your feelings.)

_____

_____

_____

_____

ACTION ITEMS

Here are specific actions you can take to implement the lessons and ideas you learned in this chapter:

1   Make a commitment to initiate more communication with your parents and in-laws. Use whatever mode of communication feels comfortable, from writing an email to making a phone call to planning a visit.
2   Research your family trees on both sides. Learning the stories of your ancestors connects you to family legacies.
3   Register for a parenting class or workshop together.
4   Practice using the trick of narrating subtitles to explain your parenting choices to one another.
5   Plan a child-free vacation or date night. Try to enjoy each other's company without talking about your children!

REDEFINE RELATIONSHIP ROLES

The gendered roles of partner—husband, wife—are often fraught with expectations that come from our families of origin, our culture, books and movies, and the mentor couples we know. Expectations of relationships can help us strive for what we value, or they can undermine our ability to accept reality.

But husband and wife aren't the only roles we play in marriage. The other roles we play are like following scripts—they come with rules, expectations, and behaviors. We take on roles in relationships based on our innate skills, our learned experience, and the expectations of our partner. Some roles come naturally to us; others seem required but do not feel comfortable. In this way, relationship roles can be like jobs: Some jobs are easy, and others are hard. And these roles can strengthen your sense of partnership or undermine your teamwork.

Take a moment to fill in the areas of strength and conflict from your everyday issues assessment (page 11) that will guide your focus in this step.

Step 7: Redefine Relationship Roles

Strengths _____ and _____

Conflicts _____ and _____

Relationship Roles

First, let's pay attention to the roles of husband and wife, wife and wife, or husband and husband. These are the primary roles we play in marriage, and they are the most complex. Then we'll explore the other roles you play in your relationship and how these roles either complement your natural abilities or put you outside of your comfort zone.

EXPLORE THE IDEAL QUALITIES OF A HUSBAND AND WIFE

CARLOS SAYS: *"My dad had a strong personality, and he not only took care of our own family but also helped with his brother's kids. I want to be like him in that way. And I want Janelle to know she can always count on me; I want to be strong but steady. When I think about the ideal wife, I think Janelle is pretty close! The qualities I'm thinking of are qualities she has."*

What are the ideal qualities and behaviors of the relationship role you are striving for in your marriage? Perhaps you pull from your parents' relationship or from mentor couples in your life. What do you want to emulate? What do you want to change?

_____

_____

_____

_____

What do you expect from the ideal role of your partner?

_____

_____

_____

_____

IDEAL-QUALITIES LIST

In the worksheet below, create a list of what you would consider the ideal qualities for each role. Use only as many lines as you need, and feel free to add more.

Carlos's list for self/husband included provider, strong, and emotionally steady. For the ideal qualities of partner/wife, he wrote friendly, ambitious, and dependable.

Self_____	Partner_____
_____	_____
_____	_____
_____	_____
_____	_____
_____	_____
_____	_____
_____	_____
_____	_____
_____	_____
_____	_____
_____	_____
_____	_____
_____	_____
_____	_____
_____	_____
_____	_____
_____	_____

How are your lists aligned? How are they different?

_____

_____

_____

_____

To what extent are these lists based on gender roles?

_____

_____

_____

_____

Where did you learn these ideals?

_____

_____

_____

_____

Are any of the problems in your marriage now a result of these ideals not being met?

_____

_____

_____

_____

Are you struggling with not meeting your ideals for your role in the marriage or the ideals your partner holds for you?

_____

_____

_____

_____

WHAT OTHER RELATIONSHIP ROLES DO YOU PLAY?

Listed in this worksheet are other common roles partners play in marriage. Place a check mark in the column that best describes you for each role. Add any other roles that are relevant in your marriage.

	Yes, this is me.	No, this is not me.	I wish this were me.
Adventurer			
Financial adviser			
Homebody			
Instigator			
Justice enforcer			
Manager			
Nurturer			
Organizer			
Peacekeeper			
Pleaser			
Problem solver			
Social coordinator			
_____			
_____			
_____			

Which of the roles that you play are a natural fit for you? Which do you enjoy the most?

_____

_____

_____

_____

Which roles are uncomfortable for you to play? Which would you prefer your partner to play instead of you?

_____

_____

_____

_____

Which roles are you both playing, and does this help your sense of teamwork or cause battles between you?

_____

_____

_____

_____

Which roles would you like to experiment with playing?

_____

_____

_____

_____

How can you help each other take on new roles?

_____

_____

_____

_____

WORK/LIFE BALANCE

Another important way relationship roles play out in a marriage is how you balance the roles you have at home and the roles you have at work. For some partners, playing the same role at work and at home provides consistency and stability. For example, at work you're a manager, and at home you're a manager, so one role blends seamlessly into the other. For others, playing complementary roles at work and at home provides a respite and a chance to use different skills. For example, at work you're a financial adviser, and at home your partner is the one in charge of paying the bills, giving you a break from constantly seeing dollar signs.

Although Beth and Mei-Lin work at the same art museum, their jobs are very different. Beth, one of the curators, is responsible for assembling, managing, and presenting art in the East Asian gallery. Mei-Lin is an archivist, specializing in digitizing media for public access. Beth spends her days bustling from meeting to meeting, phone call to phone call, gallery to vault to exhibition. Mei-Lin mostly sits at her desk in the museum offices, content with her camera and computer and library.

Both consider their jobs a natural fit for their personalities, but conflict comes when they make the transition to home. Beth is energized by her day and is often ready to keep that energy going by meeting friends for drinks, dinner, or a movie after work—not doing household chores like cooking, dishes, laundry, and household finances. Mei-Lin is content after a day of work and looks forward to reconnecting with Beth by making dinner together.

What does my job/work/career want from me (for example, performance and commitment)?

_____

_____

_____

_____

What do I want from my job/work/career (for example, compensation and recognition)?

_____

_____

_____

_____

What does my marriage/family want from me (for example, participation and negotiation)?

_____

_____

_____

_____

What do I want from my marriage/family (for example, belonging and partnership)?

_____

_____

_____

_____

CHORES, HOUSEWORK, AND CHILDCARE

If you and your partner are experiencing conflict about divvying up housework, yard work, or childcare tasks, perhaps you're using a strategy that doesn't work for you. Or perhaps you're using the same strategy for all the chores instead of using different strategies for different chores.

Review the three common ways couples split up chores, and see which best describes your situation.

1 Splitting chores based on who has the time to do them.
2 Splitting chores based on skills or interest.
3 Splitting chores based on traditional gender roles.

TOSS THE SCORECARD

Score keeping has no place in a healthy marriage. Scores are kept when two teams are competing against each other, but you're not on different teams—you're on the same team! Don't expect your contributions to be equal in any given moment, but do expect them to even out over the entirety of your marriage. Teamwork is so much more than an even split of daily chores; different tasks carry different weights, and different seasons of your life together allow for different contributions.

If you catch yourself keeping score with your partner, repeat this mantra: "We're a team working toward a common goal." Saying it over and over to yourself will help train your brain to focus on your partner as a *partner.*

HOW CHORES WORK IN YOUR HOUSEHOLD

Listed in this worksheet are several common household chores. For each chore, fill in who does it, whether or not that arrangement is working well, and how it might work better, if applicable. Add any other chores that need to be done in your household.

	Who Does It?	Working Well?	How It Might Work Better?
Arranging babysitter			
Arranging playdates			
Bill paying			
Booking travel			
Car maintenance			
Child meals			
Child pickups/drop-offs			
Diaper changes			
Dishes			
Dry cleaning			
Dusting			
Grocery shopping			
Laundry			
Making the bed			
Meal prep			
Teacher conferences			
Tidying			
Trash/recycling			
Vacuuming			
_____			
_____			
_____			

Teamwork: Create Household Equality

Problems around household equality and childcare tend to stem not so much from the actual divvying up of labor but from the meaning couples attribute to what they do *and* what their partners do. The perception of unequal work at home often causes resentment and anger. The following are four common unhelpful thoughts that undermine the sense of teamwork couples crave around household equality:

STATEMENT #1: "IF I WANT SOMETHING DONE RIGHT, I HAVE TO DO IT MYSELF."

JOSH SAYS: *"Heather would probably tell you that I rarely changed diapers, and that's true. I rarely did. But not because I didn't want to help! I didn't offer because every time I would attempt to, she'd either criticize how I did it, redo it herself anyway, or blame me if a diaper I had changed leaked. It wasn't worth the hassle or the negativity. If she cares so much about the way diapers are put on, she can do it herself."*

HEATHER SAYS: *"It was easier to do it myself than have to clean up the mess when he did it. Maybe I didn't really teach him, but he never figured it out. I decided I had to do it myself, but I really resented having to change all the diapers."*

Like Heather, abiding by this maxim may lead you to do all the chores, since you're the "only one" who can do them right. The more you do something and the less your partner does it, the more that cycle repeats and repeats, and the more you will have to overfunction in that area and your partner will underfunction. Over time, you will resent your partner for not helping you, but you may not realize that it was you who created the dilemma! And don't assume that your partner doesn't want to help—like Josh, it may be that they're conditioned not to.

Have you ever made this statement? In what situations? Do you believe this statement is true?

_____

_____

_____

_____

CHORE SWAP

Think of one task you usually do—for example, changing diapers, mowing the grass, loading the dishwasher, or making social plans. The next time that task needs to be done, instead of doing it yourself, teach your partner how to do it. Explain the steps, the tricks, and the insider information. Let your partner do it a few times in a row before doing it again yourself. What chores will you swap?

_____

_____

_____

_____

STATEMENT #2: "YOU TAKE ME AND WHAT I DO FOR GRANTED."

CARLOS SAYS: *"Even though Janelle is the one who usually gets all the credit for keeping our condo looking amazing and keeping our social calendar full, I often feel taken for granted. I work hard, too. I do things around the house, too. But the things I do are never up to her standards, so it's like they don't count. I know it drives her crazy, but really—a little more recognition, a little more credit, would go a long way with me. I felt never good enough growing up, and I still feel like that now."*

Once you start telling yourself that your partner doesn't appreciate or notice what you do on behalf of the family, it becomes a self-fulfilling prophecy. That's because, usually, instead of choosing to assertively share your feelings from your heart (for example, "I feel unappreciated when I work hard around the house and you don't notice my efforts"), you don't say anything at all, punishing your partner for not noticing by sulking, giving the silent treatment, or snapping with a prickly attitude. And I get it, I really do—it doesn't feel good to feel taken for granted. But instead of allowing that feeling to take over and become the reality, it is possible to choose a different approach.

EXPLORE THIS STATEMENT

Have you ever made this statement? In what situations? Do you believe this statement is true?

_____

_____

_____

_____

WEAR YOUR DETECTIVE HAT

For a 24-hour period, pay attention to every single thing your partner does for themselves, for you, or for the family. Seriously—every single thing! No matter how small, trivial, or mundane.

You're going to have to pay close attention to things that usually slip under your radar. And you may have to ask questions about what your partner did when you weren't around. Keep an actual list, not just mental notes. At the end of the day, share your gratitude for the multitude of activities and behaviors on the list.

Then switch roles: The next day it's your partner's turn to keep a list of all that you do and to express gratitude to you. It's okay if you both find yourselves doing a little more than usual. What matters is that you each express your appreciation to the other.

How does it feel to be noticed in this way? How does it feel to notice all the things your partner does?

_____

_____

_____

_____

STATEMENT #3: "YOU'RE NOT HELPING ME."

BETH SAYS: *"I remember back when we were renovating the town house, I would say this to myself and to Mei-Lin all the time. To me, it seemed like I was doing everything. Arranging contractors, making decisions about fixtures and outlet placements and paint colors. Eventually, after a night of complaining to my friends at the bar, I confronted her about it. The fight was awful. She was defensive. I was belligerent. It took us a long time to recover. And it turns out, she was actually helping. She was paying all the bills. I hadn't even realized it, because our system is that we split big stuff 50-50, but she had been quietly taking care of all of them."*

You may have read the second unhelpful thought and said to yourself, "Appreciation is one thing, but actual help is another!" And you're right—a sense of teamwork is essential to a healthy marriage, and this includes both partners helping. But "You're not helping me" undermines your teamwork, instead of strengthening it. We often assume that the stronger our feelings are about something, the truer our thoughts are that accompany those feelings. And just because we feel something strongly doesn't mean we've accurately perceived the situation.

Have you ever made this statement? In what situations? Do you believe this statement is true?

_____

_____

_____

_____

REFRAME YOUR PERCEPTION

The next time you want to say, "You're not helping me," use the phrase "The story I'm telling myself is . . ." as a way to frame your thoughts and feelings. Using the word *story* suggests to your partner that you acknowledge the way you see things *might not be true*, and that you're open to hearing a different story. For example, "The story I'm telling myself is that you're not helping me. I'm really feeling unsupported right now. You could help me by . . . ." Ask for what you need, assertively and sensitively, from your heart. How did that feel?

_____

_____

_____

_____

STATEMENT #4: "YOU SHOULD HAVE ASKED ME TO HELP."

TIM SAYS: *"I definitely help! As soon as Linda asks me, I'll do whatever she tells me to. She's in charge."*

LINDA SAYS: *"For our 30th anniversary party, I had prepared everything. Ordered the invitations, planned the menu, cleaned the house, did the shopping, prepped the meal . . . and Tim comes waltzing in from a day of playing golf. 'What can I do?' he asked me. I just stared at him. 'Set the table, please,'*

I responded. 'What plates should I use? Do you want to eat in the dining room or the kitchen?' We go back and forth a bit, and then he goes off to do it. I come in later and there aren't any napkins, there aren't any candles, and he didn't move the glass bowl I keep on the table when we're not eating there. 'You didn't mention it!' he said when I pointed these things out. But our friends were coming soon, so all I could do was just take care of it myself."

This is the other side of the previous unhelpful thought; your partner may be thinking, "You should have asked me to help" while you're thinking they don't help. Emotional labor, or mental load, is a concept that describes the experience of a partner, usually the wife, as carrying the burden not only of executing most of the housework but also *thinking about* most of the housework. One of you becomes the manager, the delegator, and the keeper of the to-do lists. The other one becomes the subordinate, the directions follower, and the abdicator of responsibility. Not carrying the mental load is less work *and* less energy. Your partner is doing the extra emotional work for you, and that can stifle your ability to function as an equal partner.

EXPLORE THIS STATEMENT

Have you ever made this statement? In what situations? Do you believe this statement is true?

_____

_____

_____

_____

MENTAL LOAD QUIZ

Explore the extent to which each of you carries the mental load for your relationship by taking the following quiz.

1 You're at the grocery store. What do you buy?
   a) I refer to my list and, with the exception of a few impulse purchases, I buy only what is on the list.
   b) I refer to my list and . . . then I remember we're out of mustard, so I grab some, . . . and then I remember we should stock up on extra paper towels because we're hosting a barbeque with friends over the weekend, so I grab two packages, and then . . .
2 You sit down at the end of the day to watch a TV show. What are you thinking about?
   a) This show is amazing! I wonder what's going to happen next?
   b) I must remember to pay the babysitter a bit extra next time; she's been so good about making sure the kitchen is cleaned up before we get home. This show is really interesting, I wonder . . . Oh! Tomorrow when I pick up the dry cleaning, there is a drugstore around the corner, so I can definitely pick up more children's pain medicine since we used up the last of it . . .
3 You're reading your email as you notice your partner coming down the stairs with a large load of laundry. What do you do?
   a) Wait for them to ask for help—they're a grown-up! They can ask.
   b) Offer to help as you get up from your chair to pick up a sock that dropped out of the pile.

If you answered mostly *a*, you probably don't carry the mental load for your family. Do you agree? Are you surprised? Review the "Wear Your Detective Hat" exercise on page 211, and compare the lists of what you do and what your partner does for your home and family. Are there tasks you can take off your partner's list? Ask your partner how you can be a better teammate.

If you answered mostly *b*, you probably carry the mental load for your family. Do you agree? Are you surprised?

3 TIPS FOR HOSTING AS A TEAM

Hosting friends for dinner or brunch at your home is a wonderful way to feel connected, yet so many couples struggle with hosting as a team. Instead of a fun-filled event, the experience can become a trigger that leaves partners feeling criticized, micromanaged, hurt, and resentful. It doesn't have to be this way! Here are three tips for hosting as a team:

1. Discuss ahead of time how you and your partner can be helpful to each other. Think about the most important things your partner can do before, during, and after the party to help the event go smoothly. If your partner keeps your request in mind and then intentionally follows through, they will demonstrate strong commitment to teamwork and will contribute to a sense of connection.

2. Create a secret signal of connection. Before the party starts, decide on a secret signal of connection you can swap with your partner—like a high five or a quick back rub. Then, when things start to get stressful at the party, make eye contact so you have each other's attention, and do your secret signal. The signal doesn't have to be elaborate, just a clear sign to each other that you are on the same team. Repeat the signal often!

3. Self-soothe in healthy ways. Inevitably, things will go wrong—your guests bring up a touchy subject, you run out of ice, or the kids wake up and one of you has to retreat upstairs to soothe them. But, ultimately, each of you is responsible for how you react in these stressful moments. Instead of succumbing to a negative attitude and snapping at your partner, try a self-soothing strategy that will help you center yourself and stay calm, such as retreating to a quiet place (the bathroom usually works) and taking a few deep breaths or drinking a glass of water.

PRACTICE HOSTING AS A TEAM

The next time you host a party or get-together, take some time before the event to talk about the three tips for hosting as a team. Make sure you follow them! Then, after the event, check in with each other. Was hosting this event less stressful and more fun than previous parties? Did you feel more connected to each other this time? What were the highlights?

_____

_____

_____

_____

Look back over the discussions and exercises in this chapter. What did you learn? What are the important new ideas for you? How will you use them to strengthen your marriage?

_____

_____

_____

_____

How are you feeling? How is your partner feeling? What are the similarities and differences in how you're feeling? (See appendix A for help with identifying your feelings.)

_____

_____

_____

_____

ACTION ITEMS

Here are specific actions you can take to implement the lessons and ideas you learned in this chapter:

1 Swap chores for a week, first teaching your partner what they need to know to do that chore well.

2 Create "coupons" for each other, offering to take over a household task you don't usually do. Cash in your coupons when you need a break.

3 Watch a movie together from an earlier era that features a married couple or romantic relationship. What do you notice about relationship roles from this time? How are yours similar or different?

4 If you have a child who is the same gender as you, write a letter to your child describing your wish for their future as a partner in marriage.

5 Use that secret signal of connection not just to help you through hosting parties. Use it throughout regular days together to foster a positive spirit all the time!

MAKE THE COMMITMENT

In this final step, I'm going to help you and your partner make the commitment to each other to take care of yourselves, take care of your marriage, and maintain your progress toward a lasting partnership. Each of you is responsible for doing your part, for finding your own happiness and joy, and for sharing a vision of the future that honors your individuality as well as your partnership.

You have the tools you need now, and you've done the hard work to restore your marriage to a place of health. But as we explore this final step together, it's important to be clear about those tools: A hammer is great for pulling out a nail or hammering one in, but it's not so great for a screw or a bolt. Use the right tool for the problem at hand! And don't let your tools become weapons. A hammer can do serious damage to walls or fingers if you're not careful. Be intentional with your relationship toolbox—take inventory of it, know which tool is for which problem, and commit to using your tools only for good.

Take a moment to fill in the areas of strength and conflict from your everyday issues assessment (page 11) that will guide your focus in this step.

Step 8: Make the Commitment

Strengths _____ and _____

Conflicts _____ and _____

Personality and Lifestyle Challenges

Understanding your own personality and the way you think and how you respond helps you teach your partner about you and helps you more clearly articulate what you need. When issues like depression, anxiety, trauma, and low self-esteem occur in the marriage, it is important to be honest with each other about them. These issues are often difficult to manage on your own, so work as a team to get the support you need. Common issues that bring people to therapy (either because they have the problem or their partner has the problem) are listed in the worksheet in the next exercise.

IDENTIFY CHALLENGES

In the worksheet below, place an X in the column that best describes you for each challenge listed.

	Not a problem	Sometimes a problem	Always a problem
Anger			
Diet			
Exercise			
Medical conditions			
Negativity			
Sadness			
Secrets			
Self-worth			
	Not a problem	Sometimes a problem	Always a problem
Sleep			
Stress			
Transitions			
Traumatic memories			
Worry			

TAKING BETTER CARE

What are the changes you can make in your routines and self-care that would improve your physical and mental health?

_____
_____
_____
_____

What are the ways you can help your partner make changes that would improve their physical and mental health?

_____
_____
_____
_____

What sort of support do you need from you partner to be successful?

_____
_____
_____
_____

What are the barriers to improving these issues in your life?

_____
_____
_____
_____

PRACTICE EMPATHY AND PERSPECTIVE TAKING

When one or both partners are experiencing stress, anxiety, depression, or any other distress, the skills of *attunement*, or the ways we demonstrate our partner is seen and heard as a whole person, are more important than ever. I'm going to name those skills *empathy* (the ability to connect with another person's experience, especially their feelings of pain) and *perspective taking* (the ability to accept another person's experience as their truth). Here is an exercise to help you practice these skills by "leaning in" to your partner:

PRACTICING LEANING IN

I often use the imagery of "leaning in" to describe an emotional stance in a relationship. The next time your partner is experiencing some sort of distress, use it as an opportunity to *lean in* to your partner by creating an offer for connection through empathy and perspective taking. For instance, instead of leaving the room when your partner snaps at you unexpectedly, or assuming your partner needs space when they seem like they are in a bad mood, make an offer of connection by asking "how are you feeling?" and really listening to their answer. Notice what happens.

Are you able to lean in to your partner, creating and completing offers for connection? Or are you *leaning away* from your partner, ignoring or rejecting offers for connection?

_____

_____

_____

What are the ways in which you ask your partner for connection? What keeps you from asking for the connection you yearn for?

_____

_____

_____

How do you respond when your partner leans in or leans away? How does your partner respond when you lean in or lean away?

_____

_____

_____

Rituals of Connection

Rituals of connection help you stay tuned in to each other and prioritize time together that nurtures both your individual selves and your marriage. Throughout the chapters and steps of this workbook, you've learned dozens of ways to introduce rituals of connection. Take a few minutes to flip back through the workbook to the exercises and interactions that were helpful for deepening connection and intimacy.

Another way to think about rituals of connection in your marriage is through metaphor. Think of your marriage as a medicine cabinet that is full of different options—some maintain health in our bodies, others alleviate pain, and still others cure infection. Let's name these options *vitamins*, *pain relievers*, and *antibiotics*. Each option has a different purpose, is taken for different reasons, and has different effects. Rituals of connection between partners can be categorized into these types of relief, too. Which activities do you do to preventively maintain connection (vitamins), what activities do you do intentionally to alleviate pain (pain relievers), and what activities do you do to cure more serious problems in your marriage (antibiotics)?

For some couples in my practice, a weekly date night is a "vitamin." For others, a date night is a "pain reliever." And for still others, those who are at the phase in their lives of babysitters and hectic work schedules, setting aside quality, focused time with each other is an "antibiotic."

STOCK YOUR MARRIAGE "MEDICINE CABINET"

In this worksheet, choose words from the list to stock your marriage "medicine cabinet." Add any other remedies you'd like to try as well.

Date night
Gift giving
Counseling
Kissing
Love letters
Time apart

Sex
Apology
State of the Union meetings
Holding hands
Gratitude
Couple-only vacation

Vitamins	Pain Relievers	Antibiotics

Continue Working on Your Relationship

Throughout this workbook, you have been taking important steps to heal and strengthen your marriage. If you need more support than this workbook has been able to provide, where do you turn next? What kind of counseling would be helpful: individual, marriage, or discernment? Here's a description of each.

INDIVIDUAL COUNSELING

Individual therapy is something you do *just for yourself*. It means you allow yourself time to make yourself a priority in your weekly schedule. Individual therapy is self-care and self-love, and it can be deeply healing. Your relationship with yourself sets the tone for every other relationship you have. Together with your counselor, you'll sort out your thoughts, feelings, behaviors, and goals in a safe, sensitive, and collaborative way.

Individual therapy is usually a combination of talk therapy, lifestyle changes, mindfulness techniques, and coordination of care with other professionals who may prescribe medication if appropriate. Individual counselors at my practice work from what we call a *systemic perspective*—meaning we explore the ways in which your inner life is influenced by your outer life, or most important, your closest relationships.

MARRIAGE COUNSELING

Marriage counseling requires a commitment to the relationship as well as a commitment to the work. The goal of couples therapy is to get right down to the hard work of restoring your marriage to health. Your therapist will help you process past emotional injuries, improve communication and understanding, deepen intimacy and sexual connection, and learn conflict resolution skills for a healthy and happy future.

Some marriage counselors are trained in a specific approach, such as the Gottman Method or Emotionally Focused Therapy (EFT). Other marriage counselors tailor their approach to your unique relationship and goals, using empirical research and their own experience to combine interventions that will help you repair and enrich your marriage. Choosing a licensed marriage and family therapist means you can be confident you're working with someone specifically trained to work with couples.

DISCERNMENT COUNSELING

Discernment counseling is a specific kind of short-term counseling for couples unsure about the future of their marriage. A metaphor I like to use is that discernment counseling is like the conversations you'd have with a doctor before a major operation: You haven't decided to do the procedure yet, and you want to think carefully through the risks and benefits, as well as what it might mean to not do any procedure at all.

Discernment counseling is focused on helping each partner gain clarity and confidence about a direction for the future of the marriage, based on a deeper understanding of what has happened in the marriage. The goal is not to solve the marital problems—yet—but to decide what it would take to solve them and which of three paths to take going forward: (1) attempt to restore the marriage to health through couples therapy, (2) move toward separation or divorce, or (3) take a time-out from counseling and return to the status quo.

During each session, the therapist spends time with the couple and also spends time individually with each partner. At the end of each session, each partner decides whether to schedule another discernment session or whether a decision about what to do next has been reached.

Balancing Acceptance and Commitment

The idea that you can simultaneously accept your marriage as it is and commit to making positive changes for the future may seem contradictory. *You may wonder how you can accept things as they are when you want them to be better.* I want to offer you the idea of *balance*. When you sway or dance with your partner, you're balanced on your feet while shifting your weight from one side to the other. This work of acceptance and commitment to change takes a similar kind of emotional balance that is sometimes difficult but is always important.

On one side, we have acceptance. Acceptance is full of forgiveness, grace, benefit of the doubt, and good intentions. The message is "I am okay. Right now, just as I am, I can just be." Or the message is "We are okay. Right now, just as our marriage is, we can just be." On the other side, we have commitment to change. Commitment to change is full of motivation, encouragement, willingness, and acknowledgment of shortcomings. The message is "I can try again, I can make a different choice." Or the message is "We can try again, we can make different choices."

Balancing acceptance of the now with a commitment to change in the future is the way you can both love yourself as you are and hold yourself accountable to change—the way you can relax into your marriage as enough for now and try new strategies for a healthier future. Practice accepting the now while committing to a more positive future by using the phrase "We're okay, and let's try again."

Shared Vision of the Future

As long as two partners are joined in marriage, they're going to share a future together. But how that future looks is entirely up to you! Set goals for the future that reflect both your personal goals as individuals and your joint goals as a married couple.

SHARE A VISION FOR THE FUTURE

Focus goals on the next few years: How do you want to grow as a person? What do you want to accomplish together? Are there ways you want to strengthen your family?

One of Tim's personal goals is to improve his golf game and make more use of the club he belongs to; one of his marriage goals is to travel abroad with Linda and experience adventure with her. One of Linda's personal goals is to join the faculty of the local community college; one of her marriage goals is to continue to play golf with Tim to share a common enjoyable hobby. One family goal they both share is to see their kids more often, not just at the holidays.

Self

1 _____

2 _____

3 _____

Marriage

1 _____

2 _____

3 _____

Family

1 _____

2 _____

3 _____

EXPLORE IMPORTANT GOALS

Tim and Linda have been fighting about what the next few years will hold after Tim retires, so they knew they needed to use the skills from chapter 1 and step 1 to talk about a shared vision. Tim was able to listen with his heart to the importance of a career for Linda; Linda was able to connect with Tim by sharing his passion for golf. Together, they separated the solvable parts from the unsolvable and came up with a plan: Linda teaches for the fall and spring semesters ("You can grade assignments while I play a round of golf, and then we can have dinner at the club"), and over winter break and summer break they'll plan two trips, one abroad and one within the United States ("I can't wait to see the Grand Canyon with you!").

Which goals are most important to you right now?

_____

_____

_____

_____

Which will be easy to accomplish, and which will require more planning or effort?

_____

_____

_____

_____

How can your partner participate in your individual goals?

_____

_____

_____

_____

How can each of you participate in your goals for your marriage and your family?

_____

_____

_____

_____

Are any of your goals in opposition to your partner's? How will you create a vision of the future that balances both of your goals?

_____

_____

_____

_____

MAP YOUR GOALS TOGETHER

Similar to the Venn diagram you completed in chapter 1 (page 15), this one is to map your goals together. Again, use colors to differentiate your goals from your partner's goals, placing the ones that are the same in the center section.

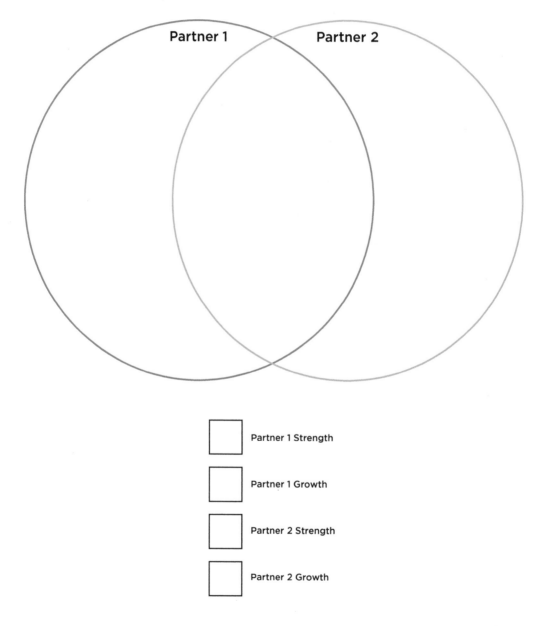

Partner 1   Partner 2

☐ Partner 1 Strength

☐ Partner 1 Growth

☐ Partner 2 Strength

☐ Partner 2 Growth

What proportion of your goals is the same, and what proportion is different?

_____

_____

_____

_____

Do your partner's goals surprise you?

_____

_____

_____

How did each of you _feel_ while sharing your lists? (See appendix A for help with identifying your feelings.)

_____

_____

_____

How well did you communicate through this exercise?

_____

_____

_____

MAKING DECISIONS

The path forward for your marriage is entirely in your hands. And you have decisions to make:

1 To what extent will you continue using the ideas and skills in this workbook?
2 Which behaviors and activities will you continue to prioritize to maintain connection?
3 Will you seek further support through counseling?

It's not uncommon for couples to get caught up in whether they're making a "right" or "wrong" decision. Using this kind of all-or-nothing thinking isn't helpful—mistakes in decision making are unavoidable, but that doesn't mean you got it wrong. Instead, think about these decisions as "course affirming" or "course correcting." Did your decision keep you on the same path or help you change paths? Do you need to alter your path after the decision, or is this the way you want to keep going?

It's also not uncommon for couples to freeze when making these decisions, not because they're afraid of making a wrong choice but because there are so many choices. Fear of missing out is a real thing, and it's true that sometimes saying yes to one thing means saying no to another. But it's actually not possible to do it all. We can't be everything in one person to our partners, and we can't be 100 percent at work and 100 percent at home. Instead, let's aim for *enough*—for getting most of what we want most of the time.

PRACTICE THE 6 STEPS OF DECISION MAKING

Use the six steps described on the next page to make a decision together. There is no shortage of paper for this exercise! Get all the words out, make lists, and journal thoroughly. Start here and use more paper as needed.

_____

_____

_____

_____

6 STEPS FOR MAKING GENERAL DECISIONS TOGETHER

All couples must solve problems and make decisions together as a team. Here is a six-step plan to help you make decisions effectively:

1. Define the problem to be solved or the situation that requires a decision. Be specific, thorough, and detailed. Include information about how this decision has been made in the past, why that solution isn't a good fit this time, and the ways each of you is feeling torn or stuck or conflicted.

2. Make a list of all possible decisions or solutions. Get creative, think outside the box, and don't censor any idea as too outlandish or unlikely.

3. For each possible decision, make a list of the factors involved. Financial cost? Time required? Emotional resources? Burden to execute?

4. For each possible decision, acknowledge what would be gained and what would be lost. What are the pros and cons? What are you saying yes to, and what are you saying no to?

5. Evaluate each possible decision from your different perspectives, as well as the different relationship roles you each embody (see page 200). Which decision feels best to you, and which feels best to your partner? What would the "manager" decide? What would the "peacekeeper" decide? What would the "adventurer" decide?

6. Look over the lists and notes of the previous five steps. Does a decision emerge as the best option, one that you both agree on? If so, give it a try! Make a plan to put the decision in place. If not, go back to step 1 at the beginning of this page and move through the steps again. Perhaps you need to brainstorm alternative solutions, or perhaps you need to more deeply examine the costs and gains. Keep digging—a decision will eventually emerge.

Taking Stock

You're almost to the end of this workbook! You've journeyed toward a marriage that is more loving, more respectful, and more joyful than it was when you started chapter 1. And you're likely feeling the benefits of the repairs, the enrichment, and the healing you've done. My hope is that you've restored your marriage to a place of health and connection, and you're enjoying deepened emotional safety and renewed commitment to a long-lasting future. So here at the end, let's take stock. What have you learned about the pain you have faced in your marriage? How have you learned to alleviate it? How confident are you that you'll be able to prevent further pain in the future? Take the assessment of your everyday issues again, and see how your answers have shifted:

REVISIT COMMON EVERYDAY ISSUES

	Was a strength, still a strength	More room to grow, but on the right track	Was a conflict, still a conflict	Mild or severe?
STEP 1: COMMUNICATION				
Expressing empathy				
Feeling heard and understood				
Compromise				
Fighting fair				
Avoiding conflict				
STEP 2: FINANCES				
Spending habits				
Saving habits				
Budget priorities				
Merging money/joint accounts				
Debt				

	Was a strength, still a strength	More room to grow, but on the right track	Was a conflict, still a conflict	Mild or severe?
STEP 3: INTIMACY				
Satisfaction				
Frequency				
Desire				
Affection				
Emotional intimacy				
STEP 4: PARTNERSHIP				
Social styles				
Friends' opinions/influence				
Balancing time together and apart				
Having fun together				
Role of technology				
STEP 5: TRUST				
Repairing connection after a fight				
Forgiveness				
Betrayals				
Health and wellness habits (food, exercise, self-care)				
Addiction or destructive habits				

continued

	Was a strength, still a strength	More room to grow, but on the right track	Was a conflict, still a conflict	Mild or severe?
STEP 6: FAMILY				
Your parents' opinions/influence				
Your in-laws' opinions/influence				
Parenting styles				
Reactivity				
Attachment styles				
STEP 7: RELATIONSHIP ROLES				
Household chores				
Childcare				
Work/life balance				
Coping with stress				
Teamwork				
STEP 8: COMMITMENT				
Personality differences				
Mental health issues				
Shared vision of the future				
Making decisions				
Rituals of connection				

How do you feel as you revisit the common issues in marriage and think about your progress?

_____

_____

_____

_____

What do you notice about how your areas of relationship conflict and strength have changed? Do they still center on a core group of steps, or are they more spread around?

_____

_____

_____

_____

Where have you made the most changes, and where have you slipped into old habits of disconnection? What do you still need to work on?

_____

_____

_____

_____

WHAT DID YOU SKIP?

It's okay! I know you skipped some of the exercises, and I know that you didn't read all of the sections. Why did you skip certain parts? Was it because the content wasn't relevant to you or your marriage? Was it because the content was too painful to explore? Was it because you lost interest in the workbook, or because you lost interest in your marriage?

_____

_____

_____

_____

Flip back through your workbook and review the sections that you skipped. Are there any you'd like to revisit and complete now? Are there any you'd like to try again? Make note of them here.

_____

_____

_____

_____

IDENTIFY YOUR MOST IMPORTANT TAKEAWAYS

For each chapter and step in the workbook, fill in which ideas, images or metaphors, skills, actions, or conversations were most helpful to you. These are the things that resonated most deeply, inspired the most meaningful shifts in your thinking or feelings, and helped you at least start to heal the damage that had been done.

CHAPTER 1: _____

_____

_____

_____

_____

CHAPTER 2: _____

_____

_____

_____

_____

STEP 1: _____

_____

_____

_____

_____

STEP 2: _____

_____

_____

_____

_____

STEP 3: _____

_____

_____

_____

_____

STEP 4: _____

_____

_____

_____

_____

STEP 5: _____

_____

_____

_____

_____

STEP 6: _____

_____

_____

_____

_____

STEP 7: _____

_____

_____

_____

_____

STEP 8: _____

_____

_____

_____

_____

WRITE A LETTER TO YOUR PARTNER

It's time to write to your partner in marriage. Pull from all you've learned in this workbook and feel free to add your own paragraph at the end.

Dear _____,

We met when I was _____
and you were _____.
Our relationship was characterized by _____
_____ and
_____.

People said we'd _____
_____.

When we got married, _____
_____.

Even though things have been hard for us, like _____
_____ and
_____,

I feel _____
_____

about the work we've done to repair and enrich our connection.

With you, I am learning _____
_____

about marriage. With you, I am learning _____
_____

about commitment. And with you, I am learning _____
_____

about myself. Thank you for _____
_____.

I wish _____
_____

for us in our marriage. I hope we _____
_____.

I can't wait for _____
_____.

With deep love and deep gratitude,

_____

One way many couples choose to signify a renewed commitment to each other is to celebrate by renewing their vows. Use the following questions to guide the planning of a vows renewal ceremony:

Who should be invited (for example, just the two of you, children and close family, friends and mentors)?

_____

_____

_____

_____

Where should it be held (for example, your home, where you were first married, your favorite vacation spot)?

_____

_____

_____

_____

What should you say (for example, the same text from your first wedding, revised vows based on what you've learned, new promises to your children or family)?

_____

_____

_____

_____

What rituals should you include (for example, ring exchange, either new or originals engraved, meaningful readings or music; unity ceremony)?

_____

_____

_____

_____

Look back over the discussions and exercises in this chapter. What did you learn? What are the important new ideas for you? How will you use them to strengthen your marriage?

_____

_____

_____

_____

How are you feeling? How is your partner feeling? What are the similarities and differences in how you're feeling? (See appendix A for help with identifying your feelings.)

_____

_____

_____

_____

ACTION ITEMS

For this final section of the workbook, it's up to you to decide what specific actions you can take to implement the lessons and ideas you learned in this chapter. You have the skills and tools you need! You can recommit to particularly helpful action items from previous steps, or you can create your own. What would be most meaningful to continue the work of not only this step but the whole workbook?

1 _____

2 _____

3 _____

4 _____

5 _____

CONCLUSION

Thank you for committing to this journey with me. It has been my sincere honor to help you repair and enrich your marriage through the relationship-building exercises and conversations in this workbook. I hope you feel more prepared to face the world together as a strong, connected couple.

It's time to say goodbye to the people who, by example, made real the work of part 1 and part 2, and who demonstrated the power of the Eight Steps to transform marriages.

JOSH AND HEATHER

"We made it through to the end, but honestly, we're still struggling. Although we have new skills, and we're doing our best to practice new ways of communicating, we're still feeling disconnected. We're more aware than ever of our conflicts. Both of us are worried about our future."

If you identified most with the issues, situations, or feelings of Josh and Heather throughout the workbook, revisit steps 1, 5, and 7, plus chapter 2. *How therapy can help:* Have you considered seeking support from a marriage counselor to help you navigate the path forward?

CARLOS AND JANELLE

"Thank goodness we found our way to this workbook! All we needed were specific skills, new ways of thinking about our problems, and a renewed commitment to each other (and lots more practice). We're doing better than ever—and even the people in our lives can tell."

If you identified most with the issues, situations, or feelings of Carlos and Janelle throughout the workbook, revisit steps 1, 2, and 6, plus chapter 1. *How therapy can help:* Have you considered seeking support from a marriage counselor to reinforce your already strengthened partnership?

BETH AND MEI-LIN

"We are both feeling more confident than ever in our relationship, and we can't wait to get married. We learned a lot about communication and are much more aware of each other's feelings, needs, and wants—and we're much better equipped to handle conflicts in our future as a married couple."

If you identified most with the issues, situations, or feelings of Beth and Mei-Lin throughout the workbook, revisit steps 1, 3, and 4, plus chapter 1. *How therapy can help:* Have you considered seeking support from individual counselors to help you develop insight into your own mind and emotions?

TIM AND LINDA

"We've been through so much in our long marriage already, and now we're truly excited for the decades to come. We feel reenergized, reconnected, and recommitted. (And sex is better than ever!) We weren't sure what to expect, but we've learned so much from this workbook."

If you identified most with the issues, situations, or feelings of Tim and Linda throughout the workbook, revisit steps 1, 3, and 6, plus chapter 2. *How therapy can help:* Have you considered seeking support from marriage counseling to help you transition your family into a healthy future?

I want to leave you with a final metaphor: A well-balanced marriage contains the four elements of nature that are all around us—fire, water, air, and earth.

Fire. It is hot and bright. It can be dangerous like the fire of anger or passionate like the fire of intimacy. Fire can keep you warm when it's safely contained or burn your house down when it's not. Be careful with fire.

Water. Like an ocean or a pool, you have to choose to get in the deep end or the shallow end, or not get in the water at all. It is a choice to keep each other afloat, to buoy your partner in times of sadness or hardship, to wash away hurt feelings and start again clean. Be intentional with water.

Air. Air is the space between you, and even though you can't see it, it is charged with energy, with emotion. Air carries your words, and it transmits your gaze. Through it you interact with the world around you as individuals and as a couple. Be sweet with air.

And finally, earth. The ground beneath your feet, the earth stabilizes you. It carries your memories, and on it, you build your homes. The earth grows your dreams, it connects you with the people you love, and it connects you to the greater good of humanity. Be wise with earth.

Dedicate yourselves to balancing these forces within your marriage. Remember that you will be tested by the daily routines of life, by chance and by circumstance. Remember that the full cycle of the seasons of life will repeat over and over: birth, growth, aging, decay, and rebirth. Remember that together you must encounter life's sorrows no less than its sweetness, its frustrations along with its graces.

My greatest wish for you is that you stretch your love large enough to embrace whatever life brings. Let your love fill you, surround you, comfort you, and protect you. Let your hearts truly be safe with one another. Be generous in expressing your love. Be open to receiving love from your partner. Be flexible and forgiving, and always tenderly invite each other to learn from mistakes. And, in the hardest of times, remember to reach for the best parts of yourselves.

You are strong on your own. You are strong together. And one is not stronger than the other.

May love grow between you, ever deeper, ever sweeter, with each passing day.

APPENDIX A

Feeling Words

Accepted	Criticized	Grumpy	Needy	Resentful
Alarmed	Curious	Happy	Nervous	Sad
Angry	Defeated	Hopeful	Numb	Sarcastic
Annoyed	Depressed	Hurt	Open	Scared
Anxious	Devoted	Impatient	Optimistic	Self-pitying
Appreciative	Distressed	Involved	Overcome	Sexy
Ashamed	Empowered	Irritated	Overwhelmed	Silly
Bitter	Energized	Joyful	Pessimistic	Strong
Brave	Foolish	Kind	Playful	Supportive
Calm	Friendly	Lost	Powerful	Sympathetic
Cautious	Frustrated	Loving	Proud	Tired
Cheerful	Grateful	Lucky	Purposeful	Understanding
Concerned	Grieving	Moody	Relieved	Upset
Connected				

APPENDIX B

Assess Your Marriage for Abuse

To assess your marriage for intimidation, violence, or abuse, read the following statements and answer True or False.

T / F   My partner has used force during an argument (for example, pushing, slapping, grabbing).

T / F   My partner has locked me out of our home.

T / F   I feel pressured to do sexual behaviors that make me feel humiliated or frightened.

T / F   I needed medical care after a fight with my partner, even if I didn't receive it.

T / F   I feel dread or doom when I know my partner is coming home.

T / F   My partner uses profane language that degrades my character.

T / F   My partner interferes in my life, such as my work, friendships, or activities.

T / F   My partner has threatened to hurt themselves if I ever were to leave.

To use this workbook, the answers to each question should be a resounding NO. If you answered True to *any* of them, you may be in an unhealthy or abusive relationship. Please, put this book down and seek help in other ways: Call 911, access the National Domestic Violence Hotline by phone (1-800-799-7233) or computer (www.thehotline.org), seek support from a therapist who can further assess your safety and help you make a plan, and/or share your concerns with trusted family members or friends.

REFERENCES

Sex & Intimacy

Love, Patricia, and Jo Robinson. *Hot Monogomy: Essential Steps to More Passionate, Intimate Lovemaking*. CreateSpace Independent Publishing Platform, 2012.

McCarthy, Barry. *Rekindling Desire*. Routledge; 2 edition. 2013.

Nagoski, Emily. *Come as You Are: The Surprising New Science that Will Transform Your Sex Life*. Simon & Schuster. 2015

Perel, Esther. *Mating in Captivity: Unlocking Erotic Intelligence*. Harper Paperbacks; Reprint edition, 2017.

Schnarch, David. *Passionate Marriage: Keeping Love and Intimacy Alive in Committed Relationships*. New Harbinger Publications; 1 edition. 2001.

Marriage

Gottman, John, and Nan Silver. *The Seven Principles for Making Marriage Work*. Harmony; Revised ed. Edition. 2015.

Hendrix, Harville. *Making Marriage Simple: Ten Relationship-Saving Truths*. Harmony; Reprint edition. 2014.

Johnson, Sue. *Hold Me Tight: Seven Conversations for a Lifetime of Love*. Little, Brown and Company; 1st edition. 2008.

Levine, Amir, and Rachel Heller. *Attached: The New Science of Adult Attachment and How It Can Help You Find—and Keep—Love.* TarcherPerigee; Reprint edition. 2012.

Weiner-Davis, Michele. *The Divorce Remedy: The Proven 7-Step Program for Saving Your Marriage.* Simon & Schuster; Reprint edition. 2002.

Self-Love

Brown, Brené. *Daring Greatly: How the Courage to Be Vulnerable Transforms the Way We Live, Love, Parent, and Lead.* Avery; Reprint edition. 2015.

Doyle, Glennon. *Love Warrior: A Memoir.* Flatiron Books; Hardcover edition. 2016.

Huber, Cheri. *That Which You Are Seeking Is Causing You To Seek.* Keep It Simple Books; 1st Edition. Edition. 1990.

Sincero, Jen. *You Are a Badass: How to Stop Doubting Your Greatness and Start Living an Awesome Life.* Running Press; 1 edition. 2013.

Welwood, John. *Perfect Love, Imperfect Relationships: Healing the Wound of the Heart.* Trumpeter. 2007.

Self-Exploration

Duhigg, Charles. *The Power of Habit: Why We Do What We Do in Life and Business.* Random House; 1 edition. 2012.

Epstein, Mark. *Going to Pieces without Falling Apart: A Buddhist Perspective on Wholeness.* Harmony; Reprint edition. 1999.

Lerner, Harriet. *The Dance of Intimacy: A Woman's Guide to Courageous Acts of Change in Key Relationships.* Harper Perennial; 1st Printing edition (1990)

Siegel, Daniel. *Mindsight: The New Science of Personal Transformation*. Bantam; Reprint edition. 2010.

Tavris, Carol, and Elliot Aronson. *Mistakes Were Made (but Not by Me): Why We Justify Foolish Beliefs, Bad Decisions, and Hurtful Acts*. Mariner Books; Revised, New edition. 2015.

Navigating Hardship and Pain

Bridges, William. *The Way Of Transition: Embracing Life's Most Difficult Moments*. Da Capo Lifelong Books. 2001.

Chodron, Pema. *Living Beautifully: With Uncertainty and Change*. Shambhala Publications. 2012.

Kingma, Daphne Rose. *Coming Apart: Why Relationships End and How to Live Through the Ending of Yours*. Conari Press; Reprint edition. 2012.

Paleg, Kim, and Matthew McKay. *When Anger Hurts Your Relationship: 10 Simple Solutions for Couples Who Fight*. New Harbinger Publications; 1 edition (November 9, 2001)

Spring, Janis Abrahms. *How Can I Forgive You?: The Courage to Forgive, the Freedom Not To*. William Morrow Paperbacks; Reprint edition 2005,

RESOURCES

Programs/Retreats

The Daring Way · www.thedaringway.com
The Daring Way™ is a highly experiential methodology based on the research of
Dr. Brené Brown.

Prepare-Enrich · www.prepare-enrich.com
The mission of Prepare-Enrich is to equip marriage champions, couples, and families
with evidence-based skills and insights to foster healthy relationships.

Websites

***The Art of Manliness* · www.artofmanliness.com**
Online magazine for men that explores relationships, marriage, and parenthood,
among other topics.

***A Cup of Jo* · www.cupofjo.com**
Online magazine for women that explores relationships, marriage, and parenthood,
among other topics.

***The New York Times* Modern Love · www.nytimes.com/column/modern-love**
Essays submitted by real people about love in modern relationships.

Podcasts

Dear Sugars • www.nytimes.com/podcasts/dear-sugars
A radically empathic advice show hosted by Cheryl Strayed and Steve Almond.

The Heart • www.theheartradio.org
The Heart is an audio art project about intimacy and humanity.

Where Should We Begin • www.estherperel.com/podcast
Advice on relationships and sexuality.

Apps

Couple: The App for Two • www.couple.me
Memory sharing, private messaging.

Gottman Card Decks App • www.gottman.com/couples/apps
Conversation topics to deepen intimacy.

Headspace • www.headspace.com
Meditation made simple.

Kindu www.kindu.us/#intro
Sexual exploration.

Mint • www.mint.com
Budgeting and bill paying.

INDEX

ACKNOWLEDGMENTS

Writing this workbook has been a dream come true. Thank you to my editor, Susan, for her patience and encouragement, and thank you to all of the staff at Callisto for believing in this project and believing in me. Thank you for making it possible.

So many people have contributed to my development as a marriage and family therapist, and to the creation of this book. First, thank you to my clinical professors and supervisors, with whom I found my voice as a marriage and family therapist. Thanks especially to Laurel, who taught me personally the value of metaphor, and to Carol, who personally taught me the value of leadership. Many, many thanks to my marriage and family therapy colleagues who have become my dear friends, including Jessica, Lauren, Rachel, Kailee, Brittany, Jennifer, Leanne, Dawynea, Kirsten, Erin, Tiffani, Kate, Vienna, Jenni, Caryn, Jocylynn, Kaitlin, Anna, Lindsey, Nina, and Laura. Each of you have taught me something meaningful about the power of therapy to transform relationships. I also want to thank the many voices in psychological and relationship health whose books, articles, seminars, podcasts, and research inform and inspire my practice.

I use so much of my own heart in my work with clients, so the people in my personal life also deserve sincere thanks. Thank you to the women and men who have taught me the power of love and friendship, including Melissa, Gail, Jackie, Michele, Jill, Kat, Allison A., Allison M., Natale, Ashley, Amy, Faye, Kristin, McKay, Jo, Allison C., Jason, and Mike. Thank you to my boys, John and Ethan, for making motherhood a joy and an adventure. Thank you to my family for their legacy of partnership and parenthood. Thank you to my parents, Walter and Elizabeth, for everything.

My deepest gratitude is reserved for my husband, Alex. Thank you for keeping my dreams as important as your own, and for being my light when life is dark.

ABOUT THE AUTHOR

 **Dr. Emily T. Cook** is a licensed marriage and family therapist in Maryland. Her private practice, Emily Cook Therapy, is a thriving group of marriage and family therapists who specialize in helping people repair and enrich their relationships. Couples who are committed, engaged, married, on the brink of separation, new parents, and individuals and families with relationship challenges benefit from her expertise in deepening connection and restoring healthy interactions. Dr. Cook earned her Masters and PhD from the University of Maryland, College Park, in marriage and family therapy and family science. Her leadership and advocacy on behalf of marriage and family therapists advances the profession and ensures high-quality help for couples, families, and individuals seeking relationship therapy. She lives with her family in the Washington, DC area.

CPSIA information can be obtained
at www.ICGtesting.com
Printed in the USA
JSHW051651050921
18420JS00002B/9